Success Leaves Footprints

Walk a mile in shoes of the successful people

David Lindahl
Harry Hatch
Jeff & Shari Kissee
Greg Johnston
Diane Bowman
Joe Milunas
Lane McGhee
Jeff Lindahl
David Flores
Saul Alarcon

For general information on our other products and services, please contact our Customer Care Department at 781-982-5700

David Lindahl, Harry Hatch, Jeff & Shari Kissee, Greg Johnston, Diane Bowman, Joe Milunas, Lane McGhee, Jeff Lindahl, David Flores

Success Leaves Footprints
Walk a mile in shoes of the
successful people

ISBN 978-0-692-46914-9

Table of Contents

How To Time The Real Estate Market For Maximum Gains!

David Lindahl

Whenn you mention market timing, most people think of the stock market. But what if I told you that you could become wealthier, faster if you learned to recognize which phase of the cycle any real estate market is in and then you based your buying and selling decisions to maximize the advantages of each cycle.

What if you discovered that, if you learned to recognize just one particular phase of these cycles and only invested in markets that were in this one phase, you would be literally guaranteed to obtain the maximum amount of success in the shortest amount of time? The possibility of millions of dollars in a very short amount of time.

Read this chapter to its very end and you will realize how to do just that.

There are two types of real estate investors, institutional investors and entrepreneurial investors.

Entrepreneurial investors are people like you and me who buy real estate and either flip it for a profit or hold it long term for appreciation and cash flow. The problem with most entrepreneurial investors is they only want to invest in their own "back yard" and they "fall in love" with their properties and hold them forever.

When this happens, their return on equity (the return you are getting from the equity that you have in your property) gets lower and lower as your equity get larger and larger.

Most people think that it's good to have a large amount of equity in their properties but what they don't realize is that they could use that equity to acquire larger properties, creating larger cash flows (spendable income) and thus creating even larger and larger equities.

The Institutional investor's entire strategy is based on "rolling" their equity into larger and larger appreciating assets. Doing this allows them to make the most amount of money in the shortest amount of time.

When you as the entrepreneurial investor starts thinking like the institutional investor, you begin to make the journey to attaining enormous wealth and it all begins with understanding the market cycles of real estate and the advantages that multi-family ownership has over single family ownership.

Before we talk about the different market cycles, let's compare and contrast single family properties and multi-family properties. Multi-family properties have seven distinct advantages over single family properties.

They are:
1) Greater Cash Flow
2) Less Risk
3) Economies of Scale
4) Less Competition
5) Ability to Hire Professional Management
6) Bigger Pay Days
7) Easier to Get the Money

1) The first is cash flow. Cash flow on a multi-family property is always greater than that of a single family. Simply because you have more rental units, more units means more rents coming in. Your average unit may bring in a profit of $300 per month.

If you have one unit (a single family) that's only $300 per month. If you have 10 units, that's $3000 per month. Hmmm, let's see…. $300 or $3000? That's a no brainer!

2) The more units you have under one roof, the less risk you have. If you have a single family house and you lose your tenant, you've lost 100% of your income. In some instances, this could be your entire profit for the year. If you had a ten unit building and lost a tenant, you still have nine rents coming in to pay your expenses and to give you cash flow (spend able income)!

3) Economies of scale favor the multi-unit buildings. If you have ten single family houses opposed to one six family, you'll have six roofs that need to be replaced or repaired, ten lawns to be maintained, and ten tenants spread out throughout your city or town.

In your ten unit building you'll have one roof, one lawn and your tenants are centrally located. Economies of scale favor the more units you have under one roof.

4) There's a lot less competition for the multi-unit buildings than there are for single family houses. Why? Perhaps because there's not a lot of people out there teaching how to do it, and there are plenty of real estate guru's making flipping single family houses sound as easy as chewing gum in the dark. The smart investors put multi-units in their portfolios along with single family houses (institutional investors do not hold any single family houses).

5) Because of the bigger cash flows in multi-family properties, you can afford to hire management companies to

manage your tenants, thus eliminating that hassle while you go out and do what you do best (or should do best), find and finance them (with other people's money).

When you are analyzing your multi-family deals, be sure to expense for your management fees. If the property cash flows with management fees expensed then it's a keeper. If it doesn't…go on to the next one.

Your time should not be spent unclogging toilets and taking tenant calls. Your time should be spent on those things that make you wealthier…finding more deals.

6) Your pay days are a lot bigger when you finally sell your multi-family property. An apartment complex will cost more than single family houses, because of this, they obtain a greater dollar amount of appreciation as you hold the property.

For example, a $100,000 single family house, in a market that appreciates 10% will be worth $110,000 while a ten unit property worth $600,000 in the same market (10% appreciation) will increase to $660,000 ($600,000 x 1.10 = $660,000). That's $60,000 more money in your pocket!

If you bought both properties with little or no money down, you're much better off owning the ten unit building.

7) It's easier to get the money for the larger properties. If you go to a bank to get financing for a single family property, the bank is going to take a good look at you, your history and your credit worthiness. Then they will make a decision based on credit scores and income ratios.

When you go to the bank looking to finance large apartment buildings, the bank is concerned primarily about the property. What condition is it in, where is it located, how is the market and most importantly….is it cash flowing. The bank qualifies the property first and then takes a look at you as an afterthought.

Banks even grant "non-recourse" financing. This means that the bank does not require you to sign personally for the loan! Imagine taking out a mortgage on a million dollar property and on being personally responsible!

As you can see, there are many different advantages that apartment buildings have over single family houses. That's not to say to stop flipping single family houses for chunks of cash! On the contrary, keep getting those chunks but look to create your real wealth by buying and selling apartment buildings, based on the different phases of the real estate cycle.

There are four major phases of the market cycle;

1) Seller's Market Phase I
2) Seller's Market Phase II
3) Buyers Market Phase I
4) Buyers Market Phase II

Each one of these phases has particular strategies that you should be using to maximize your wealth. Using the wrong strategy in the wrong phase could be disastrous.

In a Seller's Market Phase I, property prices are rising, rents are rising, the time that properties stay on the market is near its shortest time of all four cycles, employment is growing at a good pace and demand for property is at its highest point.

Some people think that this is not a good time to be buying. Actually, it's always a good time to be buying real estate, as long as you use the right strategies.

This market is the second best market to be buying in. There is still a lot of upside potential in appreciating and rental growth. Demand is at its height so you know that there is going to be someone out there (usually quite a few people) who will want to buy your property.

Your strategy in this market is to buy and hold long term, flip or start long term rehab projects. This is a good market to be an investor.

In a Seller's Market Phase II, the market begins to change. This is the riskiest of all four market cycles. The time that properties are staying on the market starts to increase, employment begins to slow, and demand begins to slow. Sellers are still getting inflated prices but it's taking a lot longer to do so.

Sellers who have their properties on the market begin to realize that the market is changing so they start to lower their prices to move their property. Investors who were sitting on the sidelines waiting for the market to top off now realize that the market has topped and nervously begin putting their inventory on the market.

This causes the sellers with properties already on the market to lower their prices even more. Buyers begin to realize what is happening and they start to pull back. They begin to make lower offers, there's no more competing for properties.

Some take a wait and see attitude and leave the market completely, waiting to come back when prices have lowered.

This is the beginning of the downward cycle and eventually results in a Buyers Market Phase I.

The strategies of this the Seller's Market Phase II is to buy and sell quickly. Flip. If you're going to hold for long term, you must be buying properties with a lot of cash flow and a lot of equity. You'll need this to sustain you through the next phase of the market.

You'll want to focus on motivated sellers because most sellers still think they can get the inflated prices of the previous phase. There are not as many deals in this phase but the good news is the deals that you get will have a lot more equity in them. This is because we have just gone through a phase of rapid appreciation.

As we enter the Buyers Market Phase I prices of properties continue to decline, properties stay on the market for longer and longer periods of time, unemployment reaches its lowest levels, the market is now oversupplied with properties, rents are falling and demand for real estate eventually reaches its lowest point.

Contrarian investors feel that this is the best time to get into a market. Their buy low sell high mentality has made many of them very wealthy, though the problem with investing in a Buyers Market Phase One is you don't know how low the market is going to go down.

There is an old adage in real estate investing that says, "Never catch a falling knife". Unless you are aware of changes that are happening in the area that you are interested in buying in, you are primarily investing for cash flow, since there is no appreciation in this market.

You must have enough cash flow to see you through further downturns in the market. When you're flipping properties in this market, you want to base you buying numbers on a resale price that is below market. That is so you can sell the property and get your money back so you can go out and do it again.

You'll want to check with the Economic Development Committee in the city that you plan on investing in. Ask them what they are doing to attract new jobs to the area. Jobs are the main reason that a city begins to recover. Usually, cities offer tax incentives and abatements for companies to move to their area.

This creates jobs, with the jobs comes a migration of people, and with the people comes demand for apartments. We all know what happens when demand increases…prices go up. Because we are investing in income properties, this increases the value of our properties.

So this is the first sign of a recovering market. If you know that jobs are coming (it usually takes a company 1 – 3 years to move) before anyone else does and start buying real estate in that area, you're going to hit a home run!

This is when you should be investing heavily in a Buyers Market Phase I. As those jobs begin enter the market place and the people migrate in, the city begins to enter a Buyers Market Phase II.

This phase is the millionaire maker! When you find a market that is in this phase or recognize that your city is in this phase, you want to scoop up as many properties as you can! In a very short time of holding these properties, you will be financially set up for life! This is the market that we at Creative Success Alliance specialize in locating throughout the United States.

In a Buyers Market Phase II, the market has made the transition. Prices are no longer falling and they have begun to slowly increase. Rents have begun to slowly increase along with occupancies and job growth. Properties that once sat vacant and boarded up are now being rehabbed.

The market is beginning to appreciate and will continue to appreciate at faster and faster rates.

The strategy when buying properties is pay the seller at or close to asking price. No need to haggle, as long as the property is cash flowing, your rents and property values are about to take off! Remember, the bigger the property you own, the more money you're going to make in appreciation.

People local to the market are usually unaware of what is going on. All they know is that they have been in a Buyers Market for the last number of years and have been having a hard time selling properties. They are happy to sell to you and sometimes think you're crazy for buying!

There is a general pessimistic attitude by the locals in the market. This is good!

If you live in a market that is in a Buyers Market Phase II, after you acquire all of your properties, you'll watch your rent rolls get higher and higher. You will create massive, passive, spendable income in a very short time. People have retired in 5 years or less as multi-millionaires, simply living out their days cashing their profits checks.

It that is your goal, good for you, though once you realize how to play this game you may want to seek other markets around the country and start investing in them. After you experience rapid appreciation and passive income, it become addictive. And since you know how to do it, why stop.

You may now decide to take some of your equity out of this market and put it into another market that is just at the beginning of the Buyers Market Phase II phase. At any given time there are 20 – 30 markets around the United States, regardless of what the national economy is doing, that is in the beginning phases of a Phase II.

Doing this will compound that equity and make you wealthier and wealthier. We call this "Market Hopping" and it is fast track to becoming rich.

This is how the process works. Locate a market in a Phase II. Accumulate as many properties in that market as you can until the turns into a Sellers Market Phase I.

Remember, this is the phase when demand is at its highest. Hold the property and continue to accumulate properties through this phase but be more selective in the properties you are buying because some of the "upside" has been taken out of the market.

Continue to hold until you see the market start to transition to a Seller Market Stage II. This is when you sell and invest all of your new found equity into another market.

Is there still upside in the market? Sure there is, but you want to leave a little "meat left on the bone" for the next investor. "Pigs get slaughtered".

You want to be able to sell the property in a reasonable amount of time because you're taking your profits out from this market and putting them into another market that is poise to take off.

If you try to hang around a market until all the upside has been taken out, you risk not being able to unload your property and then having to hold it through another complete cycle. The average cycle last from 8 – 20 years!

Does Donald Trump only invest in New York City? No. He buys and builds all around the U.S. depending upon the Market Cycles. Did you know that his first deal was a multi-unit complex that he bought in Ohio? Why? Because it cash flowed and it was in a Phase II.

Start thinking like an institutional investor, use the strategies of the market cycles when you are buying in your own back yard and you will become wealthier faster. And above all else, Trump said it best, "If you're going to think, you might as well think big"

David Lindahl, also known as the "Apartment King" has been successfully investing in apartment buildings and single family homes for the last eighteen years.

For a complimentary five-part, on line training, that will show you how to create $9,700 a month positive cash flow without dealing with a single tenant" just go to:

www. davesystem.com …..It's FREE!

Taking Charge of Your Destiny While Being Successful In Real Estate Investing

Harry M. Hatch

From Baby Boomers To Real Estate Entrepreneurs

W ho would not want to take charge of their destiny, no matter where they are in life? With a lifetime of experiences to guide them and plenty of resources now available, for many baby boomers, people born between 1946 and 1964, there is no better time to enter the real estate entrepreneurial world than today.

Baby boomers comprise nearly half the country's self-employed workers (~7.4 million) and their entrepreneurship numbers are growing year after year. Statistics show us 23.4 percent of entrepreneurs are between the ages of 55 and 64. It's interesting that the primary age groups for owning multiple properties are those above the age of 55.

Those most likely to own more than one residential property are more motivated to prepare for retirement, looking to build a passive income, and prepare for a time when they will no longer have to work; or perhaps a time when they will not be able to work.

Unlike their parents, who sought and could afford early retirement, many baby boomers will work well into their 60s. The census estimates 78+ million baby boomers today. Baby boomers are the richest age group in both real estate net worth as well as savings and investment accounts. America's baby boomers are facing a serious housing crunch, with many expected to struggle to afford their homes come retirement. As a result, baby boomers tend to be much more interested in real estate investing than their younger counterparts.

Baby Boomers and Real Estate Investing

One of the primary benefits of real estate investing is the ability to create multiple streams of income, which can be secured by a type of collateral that falls into a critical group of basic human needs. This fact makes multifamily real estate an enduring investment that will always be in demand.

At present, the baby boomer generation is redefining retirement, shunning the conventional traditions of retiring, staying involved, continuing to contribute, and following their passion. When it's all said and done, baby boomers have a major challenge on their hands, as keeping up with inflation and ensuring they have an adequate retirement income will not come as easy as it once did.

Reasons for Becoming an Entrepreneur

Given where the economy has been and where it may be going, there are several reasons for baby boomers to become an entrepreneur focused in real estate sooner vs. later.

- We are healthy with many years ahead of us.
- We want to stay involved and engaged.
- We enjoy generating extra income.
- We want the independence and flexibility that comes from working for our self.

- We can do business from home while using the internet.
- We will not be discriminated against because of our age.

The Art of Entrepreneurship

Sure, anyone can say that they are or became an entrepreneur, but if you want to become a successful entrepreneur, you must live and breathe the mindset of a successful entrepreneur.

- Mitigate your risk
- Realize that you cannot do it by yourself
- Leverage the experience of others
- Team up with an experienced partner(s)
- Make money while you are sleeping
- Become a passive investor
- Be SEC (Securities and Exchange Commission) compliant

Should You Be A Passive or Active Investor?

Based on the answers to the questions below, you may decide passive real estate investments are the way you want to invest in your portfolio:

- What is your real estate investment knowledge and skill level?
- How much money do you have available to invest?

- How much time do you have available and want to dedicate to investing?

  o Those in a different profession may want to further increase their income and wealth with real estate in a way that doesn't interfere with the career they love. Others may not like their current job or career path, and want to start creating income to replace their salary.

  o For some real estate investors it's an "end game" goal. They want or need to be hands on and involved in every detail now (perhaps to build up capital), but "later" they want to stop and live off the income from passive investments.

  o For other real estate investors it's about diversification. Perhaps they are heavily involved in single family home flipping, but want to diversify into another asset class.

  o For many it may be that they have a retirement account and are looking for an alternative to the stock market.

Benefits of Being a Passive Investor

Unlike active investors who have to find great investment properties, monitor the property, and deal with tenants, toilets, and trash, the passive investor works with a partner(s) and allows the partner to do all the hands on work (the dirty work).

A Passive Investor Does Not Require Specialized Knowledge

Normally, if you wanted to invest in income producing properties, you would have to spend hours educating yourself. There are many great books on the subject of real estate investment, but it would take months of research to learn what you need to know to effectively invest in real estate.

A Passive Investor Does Not Require Specialized Training

No matter how many books you read or have read, you still need actual experience under your belt before you start to become a successful real estate investor, which may mean several poor or failed deals before learning what works and what does not.

If you are interested in passive real estate investing, the first step is to find a great partner. Maple Leaf Management Group, LLC, is one such partner and we would be delighted to share with you insider access to vetted real estate investments.

With Maple Leaf Management Group, LLC, you have the resources, guidance, and opportunity to be invested in the real estate market. Now is your chance to take control and become the next real estate mogul.

Why Should You Invest In Real Estate?

There are many reasons why you should invest in real estate. However, below are the top reasons you should consider when looking to invest in any market space.

- Inflation (protection from it)

- Appreciation (making sure it's positive)

- Cash Flow (allow others to pay down the mortgage while providing you with cash flow)

- Proven - real estate is a giant industry and accounts for a substantial part of wealth creation in the world

- Real estate is a special class that can make your money work for you because it is a hedge against inflation

Maple Leaf Management Group, LLC

Maple Leaf Management Group, LLC, is a private investment company committed to collaborating with investors, mutually beneficial businesses, projects, and infrastructures that add value to their communities. The company was formed in 2008 and provides a full range of services.

The company works with each client to customize a financing or collaborative strategy that best suits their needs and vision, while carefully matching screened borrowers with lenders to create sound, win-win deals.

Our company has developed a comprehensive system to attract, analyze, process, and execute all deals in an efficient and reliable manner. Since its inception, the company has focused on renovating and improving communities with the purpose of giving back.

As a result, we work together with likeminded individuals to form a team to execute deals based on these principals. One of our partners is involved in every transaction to ensure consistency throughout the lifecycle of the deal.

Our Mission

Bring small and large investors together so they can achieve the same buying power and benefits enjoyed by larger investors in the purchase of commercial real estate. Several investors commit to purchasing an interest in a specific property.

What We Do

- Find great deals
- Locate emerging markets
- Partner with other investors
- Protect the investor's assets
- Asset management
- Create passive income for our investors
- Create profit for our investors

Why We Stand Out In Real Estate Investing

- Excellent profits

- Instant equity

- Our systematic system for overseeing the deals

- Receive the kind of returns you would not expect from a safe investment

Our System

We are the active investor and the Maple Leaf Management Group, LLC system involves eleven steps. Ten of the eleven steps are handled by our team of professionals, leaving only a single step for the passive investor to take.

1. Find great deals in the right market

2. Analyze the deal

3. Structure the deal

4. Perform due diligences

5. Present the offering to our investors

6. The investor must decide if the offering is right for them

7. Protect our investor's investment

8. Acquire the property

9. Manage the property

10.Issue quarterly checks

11.Return all the investor's investment upon sale of the property

Find Great Deals in the Right Market

Real estate is a cyclical business and its cycles will go up down for periods of time. Since real estate is a cyclical business, you must learn what to do in the various market cycles. The key is to know what to do in each specific market cycle and to match your buy and/or sell strategy to the market cycle at the time.

One of the reasons why people do not do well in real estate is because they fail to buy or sell in the right market. If you are not buying real estate at a discount and selling at or almost at premium, you are probably making a big mistake.

It does take expertise in finding the great deals that will produce instant equity and cash flow, which is the first step in the Maple Leaf Management Group, LLC system. We spend hours analyzing various markets around the country, investigating many properties, and then we work the financials until we are sure the investment will offer a good return. We find our best opportunities in the various emerging markets located throughout the USA.

Analyze the Deal

Analyzing the deal is one of the most critical components to ensure you do not waste your time and energy looking at a bad deal. There are several ways to quickly know if the deal is worth additional time and effort after the first pass through.

Gathering the Information

- Property Details: Information about the physical design of the property, including number of units, square footage, utility metering design, etc.

- Purchase Information: Basic cost information about the property you are considering, such as the purchase price, the price of any rehab or improvement work you will need to do, etc.

- Financing Details: Details of the loan you will obtain to finance the property, which may include total loan amount, down payment amount, interest rate, closing costs, etc.

- Income: Detailed information about the income the property produces, such as rent payments.

- Expenses: Detailed information about costs of maintaining the property, including such things as property taxes, insurance, maintenance, etc.

Assessing the Property Expenses

In general, expenses break down into the following items:

- Property Taxes
- Insurance

- Maintenance (estimated based on age and condition of property)

- Management (if you choose to employ a professional property manager)

- Advertising (to advertise for tenants)

- Landscaping (if you hire a professional landscaping company)

- Utilities (if any portion of the utilities is paid by the owner)

Assessing the Property Income

- Determine the total rental income and other income produced from the property

- Net Operating Income (NOI) = Income – Expenses

Financial Analysis Summary

- Analysis of the Property Using the Broker or Seller's Numbers

- Analysis of the Property Using the Historical Operating Data

- Analysis of the Property from a Pro Forma Perspective

Pro-Forma

In order to calculate cash flow, we gather the following information:

- Rent

- Property taxes

- Heat/hydro (and who pays for it – the potential tenant or the owner?)

- Electricity (again, who pays for it?)

- Garbage/sewer/recycling fees

- Property insurance (you can speak with an Insurance Broker for an estimate)

- Property management (again, you will want to research this to get an estimate)

- Maintenance of the building/property

Structure the Deal

Investing Members

- Provide the vast majority of the capital

- Receive a "preferred return" on their investment

- Receive a share of the remaining cash flow and profits

- Receive tax benefits, such as depreciation and interest deductions

Sponsor

- Provides a small portion of the capital

- Receives the same preferred return as investors on its own invested capital

- Receives a share of the remaining cash flow and profits

- May receive fees relating to property acquisition, loan financing and management

- Receives some share of the tax benefits

Mitigating Risk

The passive real estate investor's first step is to find a great partner and Maple Leaf Management Group, LLC, is one such partner. Partnering with us you will have the resources, guidance and opportunity to be invested in the real estate market.

Loan to Value Ratio

One of the most important metrics for controlling risk in real estate investing is the loan to value ratio.

Know the Players

You want to be comfortable with who you are investing with.

Title

Another important risk control metric is to ensure that the title is clean and not clouded.

Syndicating the Deal While Being SEC Compliant

Real estate syndication is "crowd funding for real estate" before crowd funding for real estate ever existed. In its most simple form, both syndication and crowd funding involve pooling capital with other individuals for a common purpose or a common goal. In real estate, that common purpose is the purchase of a property, a physical building you can see and touch.

Why Do Investors Engage in Real Estate Syndication?

The biggest reason investors participate in real estate syndication or crowd funding for real estate is access to deal flow. Not every investor has the time to search and underwrite hundreds of properties to find a gem to acquire.

What Is a Syndicator?

The syndicator allows you to buy equity in the property side-by-side with the syndicator. The property is acquired and managed by the syndicator and as an investor; you are entitled to a share to the cash flow from rents as well as a share of the proceeds when the property is eventually sold.

How We Form Syndications

The first ingredient for a real estate syndication is a "syndicator" or "sponsor". This individual or company is in charge of finding, acquiring, and managing the real estate. Maple Leaf Management Group, LLC, company has a history of real estate experience and the ability to underwrite and perform due diligence on the real estate opportunity.

The second ingredient is the other party, the investors. These are the individuals who invest with the syndicator and own a percentage of the real estate as a result. They receive all the benefits of property ownership, but they are not involved with acquiring the property, arranging financing (if there is a loan on the property) and performing day-to-day management.

The third ingredient is a third party. In many transactions, there is a third party, the Joint Venture ("JV")/Equity partner. This JV partner typically has access to a large number of investors and serves as a conduit between the syndicator and the investors. In addition to helping with the financing, they may help the syndicator with reporting, communications and even tax documentation.

Perform Due Diligence

The due diligence process is the art of inspecting the asset prior to signing the contract to purchase the property. Deals are made or broken in the due diligence phase.

Three types of due diligence to perform are as follows:

1. Financial

2. Physical

3. Legal

Due diligence is the key to investigating and discovering everything about an asset and it is a valuable way to discover what the property is all about. We perform the necessary steps to learn about a specific asset and we inspect everything possible to help ensure that we have a good understanding of what the asset is all about for our investors.

When a potential investment property has been found, the actual sale price of the property is determined after the completion of the due diligence phase. We use plumbers, electricians, contractors, and other trade resources to investigate the property while looking for hidden issues or potential risks. A certified appraiser, familiar with the community and neighborhood of the property assesses the value of the property during the due diligence phase.

The goal is to look for the details on the inside that will assist us in formulating the appropriate offer based on the actual condition of property vs. the seller's asking price and/or the appraiser's price. By conducting a detailed due diligence, we ensure an equity cushion with a solid exit strategy, if needed.

Present the Property Offering to Our Investors

Once the first four parts of our system has been completed, the next thing that remains is to find qualified investors to invest in this qualified real estate opportunity. Maple Leaf Management Group, LLC, has already scouted the property, drawn up the paperwork, and qualified the property. The offering to our investors is on a first come first served basis.

The Investor Must Decide if the Offering is Right for Them

Upon reading the offering package, the investor has to decide whether they are interested in investing in this specific investment opportunity.

Protecting Our Investors

Proper paperwork is one of the biggest keys to protecting an investor from losing money. If done right, commercial properties can maintain all the security investors might find in a bond and still gain returns higher than the stock market.

Maple Leaf Management Group, LLC, handles all the paperwork required for the real estate transaction. We make sure there are no loopholes in the mortgage, lease agreement, insurance paperwork, etc. that might leave the investor in the arms way.

Our team of professionals have seen countless deals, knows where all the loose ends are, and we are experts at tying up those loose ends.

Acquire the Property

- Close escrow

- Place the assets in a holding LLC

Manage the Property

The Property Management Association is a nationwide association. The PMA is the largest real estate management association in the nation. We oversee and manage the specific PMA who has been selected to run the day-to-day operations.

Issue Quarterly Checks

As soon as you agree to become a Maple Leaf Management Group, LLC, investor on a specific investment opportunity, you will begin receiving cash flow; money from the property begins to flow into your bank account every quarter.

Cash flow on the property depends, in part, on the amount of repairs that need to be done, but usually we will be taking over a property that has just been renovated. This renovation increases the valuation of the property and provides for minimal maintenance for 12 months and protects against repair costs from eating into the cash flow in the first year of ownership.

Quarterly checks are not the only return our investors see. As the tenants pay the mortgage down every month, the equity in the property rises. Since the equity started out at a minimum of 25%, the net worth starts out on solid ground and continues to grow from there.

We are proud to offer solid real estate investment opportunities to our investors for this lucrative real estate market that we are now experiencing.

Return the Investor's Original Investment Upon Sale of the Property

Our exit strategy is to refinance or sale the asset in 3 to 5 years. Upon the sale of the asset, the investor's original investment is returned.

Investing In Multifamily Real Estate Group Investments

There are many different types of passive investments and one structure worth talking about is the "group investment". Group investments are becoming more and more popular, especially due to recent changes in the law.

With group investments, capital from many investors is brought together to purchase a single property or multiple properties. Often a (PPM), Private Placement Memorandum (non-public offering) is used to legally structure the investment, which are also commonly referred to as syndications, or funds. The investment managers handle all details and it is a passive investment for the investor.

A passive investor who is investing and providing funding for property can expect quarterly interest payments and a final payment at the end of the loan term.

Passive Investments

Passive investments leverage the experience of other people and do not deal with banks and bank loans. In addition, the investor does not deal with tenants, toilets, or trash and make money while they are sleeping.

Leverage the Experience of Other People

Investors always have the option in any investment to go at it alone, but there is something to be said for leveraging the intelligence of the people around you. Some real estate investors devote their lives to learning the ins and outs of the market and passive real estate investing allows you to benefit from their deep education.

There are No Banks to Deal With

Dealing with banks is just plain hard. Since the economy went south, banks have started to require even more documentation and financial stability to qualify for loans and the process is both time-consuming and mind numbing.

When you are a passive real estate investor, your investment is tied to a professional private real estate investment company that already has relationships with select banks who navigate the bank financing waters on your behalf.

There are No Tenants, Toilets, or Trash to Deal With!

When you are a passive real estate investor, you do not deal with the hassles of day-to-day management or leaky faucets. The best part is you are not receiving the phone call at 2:00am for a broken gate or a kid's toy down the toilet. Instead, the maintenance person will respond to the call.

Make Money While You Are Sleeping

Passive real estate investing can be incredibly quick. You perform your due diligence, sign legal paperwork online, and transfer funds to the escrow company. The purpose of being a passive investor is to allow your money to make money for you and it literally makes money while you sleep. Primarily when investing in properties with existing tenants where there is existing cash flow, your money is working for you 24/7.

Controlling Risk

Most investors look for low risk, value creation, and high cash flow. Be it the real estate markets, the bond markets, the stock market or any other market, no investment is ever guaranteed, so do your due diligence and proceed with caution.

If you are a relatively low-risk investor and a conservative person (like we are), then you will probably appreciate the benefits of cash flow investments, as it can enable you to:

- Earn more predictable returns than the stock market (with equal or less risk in many cases)

- Earn better returns than the stock market (with equal or less risk in many cases), resulting in a higher net worth for you and your family in the long-term

- Better plan for your future by being able to predict your future returns with more certainty

- Have access to your cash flow for living expenses, retirement, and/or reinvestment, allowing you to spend or reinvest without encroaching on your invested capital

- Sleep better or at least with fewer worries, during today's economically volatile times!

Equity Investment Structures Aim At Aligning Interests

In an equity-structured investment, passive real estate allows tax-deferred cash returns that lets you keep more of your earnings.

The investments presented by Maple Leaf Management Group, LLC, are structured through our company. These structures not only give you the benefits of passive investing, they also allow for the "pass-through" of depreciation, interest expense, and other deductions that can reduce your taxable income. They represent a great investment alternative for investors who are not in a position to spend all their time searching for and then managing appropriate investment properties.

Investors will usually invest alongside a professional real estate company, often called a sponsor that will find a viable project and perform the related management chores once the property has been acquired. Such companies typically need other investors to provide some (or most) of the capital required for any single opportunity and these investors will then share in some of the project's benefits.

Although limited partnerships are sometimes used, most real estate investments are structured using limited liability companies. These entities not only provide limited liability to the investing members and usually the sponsor, they allow for the "pass-through" of tax deductions that derive from the ownership of real estate.

The structuring issues then come down to how to divide the financial benefits of the project among the investing members and the sponsor.

The Simplest Way to Invest in Real Estate

At Maple Leaf Management Group, LLC, we are proud to have developed a system of real estate investing that makes it possible for anyone to invest in real estate without any specialized knowledge or training.

Average investors do not have the time or interest to learn all there is to know about investing in real estate. However, many of them want to benefit from the great investments that commercial properties offer.

The lack of real estate investing knowledge has made real estate investment a challenge for the average investor and has been the demise of many investors. However, Maple Leaf Management Group, LLC's system alleviates this concern by allowing investors to take advantage of our team's knowledge and experience.

That is why the Maple Leaf Management Group, LLC, team has designed a system that puts the world of real estate investing into the hands of successful investors. What used to be the domain of real estate moguls, is now an investment opportunity for all.

Why Investors Invest With Us

- To earn a high rate of return in a secured investment
- We consistently hit our numbers
- Passive income stream
- IRA and 401k (self-directed) – deferred taxes
- Hands off management
- We provide timely communication
- We are conservative
- We are SEC compliant

Summary

Our Mission

To bring small and large investors together so they can achieve the same buying power and benefits enjoyed by larger investors in the purchase of commercial real estate.

One of the primary benefits of real estate investing is the ability to create multiple streams of income, which is secured by a type of collateral. This makes real estate an enduring investment that will always be in demand. Now it is time for you to:

- Take action
- Engage with a mentor
- Embrace change
- Listen to your inner voice
- Do not be afraid to ask for help
- Partner your way to success and profit
- The painful truth is that you cannot do it on your own

Entrepreneur Facts

Entrepreneur qualities include wise money management, sales closing strength, self-promotion, and collaboration. As you may know, in the business world very few are direct and completely honest. Be it customers, employees, investors, or suppliers, more often than not, you will have to spend time listening and reading between the lines.

Entrepreneurs not only must be self-motivated, but they also must possess the ability to motivate others (including themselves), even in times of stress. He or she should also be goal-oriented, able to set goals, and encourage his or her team to constantly strive to meet those goals and then stretch the goals to the next level.

Why People Invest With Maple Leaf Management Group, LLC

- Income Stream
- We are Conservative
- Hands off Management
- We Consistently Hit Our Numbers
- We Provide Timely Communication
- IRA and 401k (Self-directed) – deferred taxes
- To Earn a High Rate of Return with a Secured Investment

Our Role Is To

- Locate Emerging Markets
- Locate The Right Property
  - 100 + units
  - B, or C Property
- Partner with Other Investors
- Invest in Real Estate

- Asset Management

- Refinance or Sell The Property

- Build relationships with like-minded investors who value integrity, honesty, and trust worthiness

The Process

- Several investors commit to purchasing an interest in a specific property

- We create a "funding" to organize the investors, collect funds, invest in the complex, and distribute quarterly profits

Harry M. Hatch

From Baby Boomer to Real Estate Entrepreneur

From a blue collar worker who worked in Michigan's automobile factory and foundries, to disabled Veteran, to Silicon Valley Executive with international responsibilities for software development and delivery systems, to owner of a California construction company, and now a Real Estate Entrepreneur.

Mr. Hatch is the managing member of his company Maple Leaf Management Group, LLC. Mr. Hatch is a Business Owner, Investor, Educator and a Real Estate Investment Wealth Strategist who has a passion for helping others. His specialty is having an insider's perspective on what investors are currently doing to be successful in today's challenging markets.

Mr. Hatch is an entrepreneur and private investor with over 20 years of experience in real estate investment, private lending, and rehabbing. He was owner and COO of a private real estate investment and construction company with a portfolio of multifamily apartment units and single-family homes.

Mr. Hatch believes in helping others structure investments secured by real estate. He is currently a mentor and co-investor of multifamily apartments through his company. Mr. Hatch has extensively studied and been mentored by some of real estate industry's best, including David Lindahl, Sue Nelson, Gene Trowbridge, Robert Kiyosaki, and Dave Stech.

Mr. Hatch has a Bachelor of Science degree in Computer Science, an MBA, and is a licensed California General Contractor.

Let's Begin Our Relationship!
Contact Us Today

If you're ready to take the step on your way to high net-worth, all you have to do is contact us and we will talk with you about the opportunities.

Telephone: (916) 833-0534

Email: info@mapleleafmanagementgroup.com

New Economy, New Era, New Ways to Invest

Jeff and Shari Kissee
The Capital 8 Group

Two roads diverged in a wood, and I – I took the one less traveled by, And that has made all the difference." – Robert Frost

The Great Recession Leads to Financial Freedom

The Robert Frost quote cited above is very apropos to our story. The financial crisis of 2007-2008, which kicked off what was known as the "Great Recession", hit homebuilders very hard, and our company was no exception. The recession was a major wake up call for us, as we had been through similar challenges in the past, and we didn't want to go through that again.

Shortly before the recession hit, my wife Shari and I read a book called *Who Moved My Cheese*, by Spencer Johnson. That book helped us to realize that we needed to find a different and simpler way to achieve financial freedom. We accepted that it was not our fault that we were knocked down during the

Great Recession, but we also knew that choosing not to get back up most certainly would be our fault.

We understood that if we were to achieve financial freedom, we had to make some changes, and so we changed our focus and prepared ourselves to walk a different path.

We took to heart the words of Jim Rohn, who said, "You cannot change your destination overnight, but you can change your direction overnight." And so we began our journey in a new direction with real estate investing and The Capital 8 Group.

Everyone has a different definition of financial freedom, and that's okay if everyone has a plan for achieving that freedom. Financial freedom should be whatever each individual wants it to be. For some it is working daily, while others choose not to work at all. Some want to go on vacations, while others simply want to deepen their roots at home. What is most important is planning to ensure that you can achieve those dreams.

Having a financial plan is the vehicle that allows you to have choices, and having choices and setting achievable goals is what ultimately allows people to attain their dreams of financial freedom.

We have a friend whom we admire very much. His father retired a few years back at the ripe age of 70. He worked hard his entire life, did what most do, and saved up a nice nest egg with the mindset of having enough to be able to continue living his life on little or no income.

The reality is that besides trips to the grocery store, the doctor, and the swap meet, the father doesn't do much else these days. He lives in constant fear of dipping into his nest egg and dwindling down the principle that he spent his entire life accumulating, and so he is choosing to spend what are supposed to be the best years of a his life living a very mundane existence.

We made a choice that we were not going to retire like that man, only to watch the days tick away in boredom until one day it all ends. We decided that we were not going to live that lifestyle, but instead be active and live life to the fullest. Our mindset was that we were working hard our entire lives so that we could enjoy our golden years with no limitations, and nothing was going to stand in our way.

Our definition of financial freedom was having the passive cash flow to experience all the things we had dreamed of experiencing. Richard Kiyosaki said it best in *Rich Dad, Poor Dad* when he said "For us it means barring unforeseen cataclysmic changes, we can work or not work, and our wealth grows automatically."

My father was enormously influential in my life. He taught me to work hard for my employers and to be the first one at the office and the last one to leave. He taught me to be honest, ethical, kind, and true in all of my dealings with others. What he didn't teach me was to work smarter, to have a plan for my savings, and to set goals.

Instead, he told me that if I needed more money, then I simply had to work harder to earn more. I had believed all along that in order to someday retire, I have to save up enough money, pay off my house, and collect Social Security to supplement my income. However, when I put that plan to paper, it didn't look anything like the retirement I had envisioned for myself.

The realization that under my dad's model I couldn't come near to leading the life I wanted to live was a wake-up call for me. In order for it to work, I would have to put my very lifestyle at risk every time I drew down from my retirement savings to supplement my income.

Dad's model also was completely dependent on savings, which seemed so simple on paper but in reality was extremely difficult. Putting away 10%, or even as little as 2%, of my income served to restrict my family's lifestyle and left little or no room to handle the inevitable large and unplanned expenses.

It seemed like there was always something coming up, whether funding the kids' sporting activities, vacations, or medical expenses. Just living life itself was a never-ending depletion on our savings, and no matter how much harder I worked, the demands never seemed to become less onerous.

The only result of our working harder was that we were more tired and had less time to spend with our friends and family, which to us were the things that mattered most. We wanted to work less, not more, stress less, not more, and spend more time with our family, not less, and helping our community more, not less. What we wanted to pursue was a life full of joy and fulfillment.

There had to be a better way. We needed to take control of our finances rather than allow them to control us.

Knowing this, we began to immerse ourselves in finance, real estate, and business education. As a result, we saw a principle emerge as the solution to living the life we had dreamed of, and it was based on simply making our money work harder for us, rather than us working harder for our money. It was using our money, big or small, and doing something better with it than trapping it in a savings account that could barely keep up with inflation.

Truth be told, about the only thing we saw, as a positive in a savings account was the fact that it provided passive income, albeit a pittance of one. What we needed to do was take the principle of passive income, and increase the returns exponentially. We realized that we needed to work smarter, not harder.

Getting Meaningful Returns

> *"I believe that through knowledge and discipline, financial peace is possible for all of us." – Dave Ramsey*

During our immersion in finance and real estate education, we learned about compounding. Albert Einstein called compounding one of the greatest mathematical concepts of our time; we call it the most magical way to get rich and be financially secure!

Compounding is simply when an investment generates earnings, and those earnings are then reinvested to generate their own earnings. Where the math really gets interesting is when you incorporate the principle of compounding with higher return investments (i.e. something way north of a savings account).

Darren Hardy, Publisher and Founding Editor of *SUCCESS* magazine gives a very simple, yet profound, illustration of how compounding works. Imagine that you were given a choice to take $3 million in cash this very instant, or a single penny that doubles in value every day for a month. For the sake of example, let's say that you chose the $3 million in cash, and your friend Penny Lane went the penny route.

Five days in, your friend has a measly sixteen cents and you've got $3 million. On day ten, poor Ms. Lane is sitting there with $5.12 and you're $2,999,994.88 ahead of her. Day twenty comes along, and with only eleven days to go, your friend is looking pretty silly with only $5,242 in her pocket. Then, on day twenty-nine, things start to tighten up a bit and Penny Lane appears to be catching up with $2.7 million dollars to your $3 million.

Day 30, she's now passed you up in style with $5.4 million. Day 31 comes and Penny is laughing all the way to the bank, literally, carrying a whopping $10,737,418.24 (hopefully not in pennies!) all because she chose the compounding penny.

As you can easily see, very few things are as impressive as the magic of compounding, a concept that applies not only to our finances but also to our personal and professional lives as well.

Now that we understood the concept of compounding and the power that it had, it was time to find a way to put it to practice. It was time to create a new company and radically change the direction of our lives and those with whom we worked. And so was born The Capital 8 Group.

As we sat back and pondered our priorities and values, my wife Shari and I realized that we wanted to give back to our community and neighbors no matter what line of business we were in, and we wanted to help anyone who was interested in building an income stream of passive cash flow. In the end, what made the most sense for us given our backgrounds and our goals was to invest in residential apartment communities.

Investing in apartment communities was a way for us to build passive cash flow for our investors and for us. It would also help us to give back to our community and neighbors by improving the lifestyle and living conditions of our tenants. We wanted to provide them with safe, clean communities where they felt like they were part of a thriving apartment community that cared, rather than a cold, sterile environment.

Furthermore, knowing that ultimately, we were working smarter, and not harder, we knew that we would be freed up and have the time to personally invest in our own community and neighbors. It was the perfect solution.

We put a tremendous amount of time into developing our business model because it was so crucial to our success. There are many companies out there that invest in residential real estate, and we wanted ours to be different; we wanted it to stand out. We took the heavy lifting from our investing partners. We research, find, negotiate, purchase, and asset manage each investment from start to finish. We made investing as easy as taking your funds from one bank account to another.

That is one of the many areas that make us stand out amongst all the others. Along the way, we discovered that many of our friends and business associates wanted to know if there was a way for the smaller real estate investor to team up with the larger ones, knowing that oftentimes the returns produced by the large real estate investments were higher.

With that in mind, our company's mission statement was born:

"To bring small and large investors together so they can achieve the same purchasing power and benefits enjoyed by larger institutional investors in the purchase of apartments through passive cash flow."

Our next priority was to develop within the model a way to minimize risk by taking control of it. Fortunes have been made and lost investing in real estate. Not understanding what they were getting into has caused many investors to lose large sums of money, and we believe that many of those losses were avoidable.

As with any investment, there is always an element of risk. We, at The Capital 8 Group understand this maxim, and we make sure that our investors understand it too, but we have also structured our company to minimize those risks in every possible way.

Why Apartments? Why Now?

"The ladder of success is best climbed by stepping on the rungs of opportunity."
— *Ayn Rand*

There are many ways to become wealthy in real estate. We believe that one of the safest and most efficient ways is to buy and sell apartment buildings.

Of the many factors that mitigate the risk, some of the major ones include the following:

- Unlike office or retail space, apartments meet a basic human need: a place to live. From the dawn of man until the end of time, people require suitable shelter and apartments meet that need.

- Across most of the United States, there is a significant shortage of apartments to meet the demand.

- The ever-changing landscape of the jobs market is becoming more and more mobile. The days of staying with the same company for decades are gone, having been replaced by shorter tenures. Many young professionals are choosing the flexibility of apartment living over being anchored down to a house for this reason.

- As families recover from the Great Recession, many of them who were doubled-up and sharing space with other family members, or even other families, are moving out. The next step for most of these people is into an apartment.

- During the Recession, many college graduates were unable to find suitable jobs and were forced to move back into their parents' homes. Now that the job market is improving and recent graduates are finding jobs, they are moving into apartments.

- Many baby boomers are retiring and downsizing. For some the toll the Recession took on their retirement plans required them to sell their homes and move into an apartment in order to save money, and for others it was simply a matter of wanting a simpler, lower-maintenance lifestyle.

Another factor making apartments an attractive investment alternative is their tendency to consistently appreciate in value year after year. On the very conservative side, apartments will appreciate around the rate of inflation at 3% per year. Using that most conservative of rates of return, an apartment purchased for $1 million will be worth over $2.2 million in twenty years!

Lastly, the concept of economies of scale attracted us to investing in apartments, as opposed to single-family rentals.

Why would someone choose to invest in 100 houses, with 100 roofs, 100 furnaces, 100 lawns requiring care, and 100 water bills, when instead they could purchase a 100-unit apartment building under one roof? *(Okay, it's more like three or four roofs, but it's still well below 100!)*

By investing in a 100-unit apartment complex, an investor gets 100 tenants paying not only for the mortgage on the building, but also for all of the operating expenses of the property, and even a management company! Not to mention all of the cash flow left over after that, which in turn is paid out as dividends to the investors. What a great way to make your money work for you!

Another benefit resulting from economies of scale involves the risk of losing a tenant. With a rental house, if your tenant moves out, that property has zero income and is actually costing the owners money while it is vacant. However, with an apartment complex, that risk is mitigated due to the sheer number of tenants paying rent, and, as a result, vacancies and turnover are easier to absorb.

An apartment building can still have vacancies and generate positive cash flow, especially if the property has been properly analyzed and underwritten. A rental house cannot.

The Capital 8 Group Working For You!

We are The Capital 8 Group, and we invest in real estate assets in emerging markets throughout the United States that produce substantial excess cash flow after costs of capital and ordinary expenditures.

By understanding the markets in which we invest, we always aim to purchase at a point in a recovery cycle where we buy at a depressed price and ideally sell at a high point (more on the recovery cycle in a bit), which results in a substantially higher return on our investment.

Our market selection strategy is very simple and strategically sound. By investing in cities experiencing economic expansion, as demonstrated by job creation, population growth, and similar measures, we gain the best platform for significant cash flow and valuation improvement.

This involves buying in emerging markets that are landlord-friendly, following strict market cycle and employment criteria with multiple exit strategies.

The resultant portfolio from this strategy is a compelling investment alternative for investors seeking higher returns without assuming excessive incremental risk.

The Bell Curve and Emerging Markets

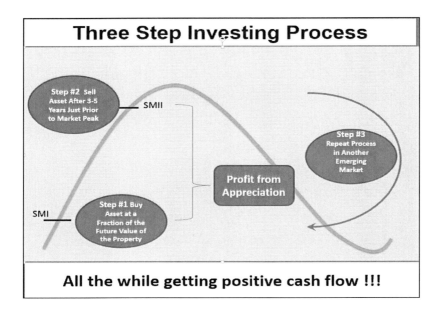

We all learned the bell curve in school. It is that graph that looks like a roller coaster ride, with its ups and downs and subtle curves at the top and bottom.

Across the nation, the bell curve represents a normal, healthy cycle that all cities and markets experience. The start of an emerging market is at the bottom of the bell curve, where it is just beginning to move upward ("SMI" on the chart).

This point in the curve is called the "recovery cycle", where jobs are being created and the market is expanding, and it is exactly that point where we like to buy properties.

Then, as the curve begins to top out, just before it reaches its highest point ("SMII" on the chart), we strive to sell the properties.

The question isn't whether or not a given market will have its ebbs and flows, or ups and downs because it will.

The question is more one of timing, and knowing when to get in the market, and just as importantly, when to get out.

Emerging Markets

"Sometimes opportunities float right past your nose. Work hard, apply yourself, and be ready. When an opportunity comes you can grab it." — *Julie Andrews Edwards*

Our business model is based on investing in emerging markets, which should not be confused with a "hot" market. The term "hot" is used to describe a market that is experiencing rapid appreciation and is likely nearing the top of the aforementioned bell curve. A hot market has already been featured in magazines and newspapers, and typically, by then, it is far too late to enter.

On the other hand, an emerging market is one where the stage is set for extraordinary growth, but it is only just beginning. The best candidates are cities with a diverse base of financially sound industries and large, stable employers. This protects the market from the loss of a particular industry or large employer much in the same way having multiple tenants in an apartment building protects the investors from having a few vacancies.

For an example of what happens to a market, that relies on a single industry for a major portion of its stability, look to Detroit or Pittsburgh. Both cities have struggled in the past because they each relied on a single industry for the bulk of their jobs and economic stability.

Today both cities are diversifying and bringing new and varied jobs into their cities and as a result, they are doing much better.

Job growth is also a major requirement, as without job growth a real estate market quickly becomes stagnant. In addition, we want to see things like vibrant shopping centers, appealing restaurants, universities, a busy airport, and high-quality roads and infrastructure. Many real estate investors overlook these factors, but we consider them crucial to a successful investment.

Ugly Properties Are Cool!

The very first property that we purchased was a portfolio property. It included apartments, self-storage units, and a retail store. It was old, run-down, had loads of deferred maintenance, and it looked just plain tired. We drove by this property once, then again, and then a third time trying to understand exactly why we should buy it.

Despite the fact that the numbers worked and it was generating positive cash flow, we were having a hard time getting over the lack of curb appeal. We had recently hired a mentor, and his advice was simply to move quickly and get the property under contract. We couldn't figure out what it was that he saw that we couldn't see, and when he explained it to us, we had what is known as an "aha moment". He told us that a building that looks tired and needs paint and landscaping is an easy fix. Upgrading the units is an easy fix, and since the occupancy was high, the property already had great cash flow.

Armed with this information, we immediately purchased the property and began our improvements. Because the property was situated on the city's main street and squarely in its path of progress, we contacted the local government and asked if there were any grants or loans available to help improve the property.

It turned out there were and we were given a grant that helped to subsidize the cost of painting the exterior of all of our buildings. In addition, the grant covered the cost of planters full of shrubs, bushes, and flowers that were placed in front of the building and maintained by the city at no cost to us. In fact, the city was so pleased that we were improving the property and the quality of life for our tenants and the area around us that it was actually hoping we would purchase additional apartments within their city limits.

The enthusiasm and support received from the city's government is a testament to the impact that small improvements have on the lives of so many citizens.

We eventually sold that property for a significant gain. Our tenants were quite unhappy to see us move on since we had improved the quality of their lives by making their community a better, more welcoming place to live. In this instance, the property happened to be in our own backyard of beautiful Denver, CO, but nowadays we go wherever emerging markets take us in the United States.

Finding Properties

Finding a good property to purchase is just as important as finding a good market. Generally speaking, we look for properties with 150 units or more if it is outside of Denver, but we will consider smaller properties if it is within the Denver Metro area. We have found around 150 units to be the optimum minimum when purchasing out of state because we can balance the costs of maintaining and managing the property to our standards with the income it generates.

Smaller properties outside of our own backyard can be a bit more difficult to justify the staffing required to ensure that they are managed to our high standards.

Apartment buildings fall into one of four categories: A, B, C, or D. An "A" property is brand new with upgrades and amenities galore. These properties are the best of the best, and fetch the highest rents by far. A "B" property is still very nice and is generally less than 20 years old.

When you get into "C" properties, they are typically around 30 years old or less, with some outdated finishes, and are usually in need of a facelift. However, they are overall structurally sound and most of the required upgrades are cosmetic in nature.

"D" properties are typically very old, run down, and have major cosmetic and structural issues that are typically very expensive to correct. In addition, as one would expect, most "D" properties are located in less-than-desirable parts of town.

As a rule, we look to invest in "B" or "C" properties situated in C+ or better areas. This is important because once we give our property a face-lift, it immediately becomes more desirable to prospective tenants, which drives higher rents and lowers vacancy.

We also look for apartment complexes that are in their city's path of progress. By talking to brokers, appraisers, and doing our own market research, we are able to figure out where the city is focusing its resources and efforts toward revitalization. Many times a city will have a master plan detailing the priority and precedence of each phase in the plan. Not only do we figure out in what parts of a particular city we want to invest, but we also figure out what parts we want to avoid.

The bottom line is that local input and research is vital to getting an accurate understanding of a city and its investment potential.

Once we've located a suitable property in an emerging market, we look for a "value add" component. This is something that we can do to the property to immediately increase its value. It could be as simple as landscaping or painting, or something more complex like adding a laundry facility or charging the tenants back for utilities.

Some of these improvements, like paint and landscaping, add curb appeal, and some like the laundry room serve to improve the lives of our tenants. What we try to avoid are major overhauls that require multiple units or entire buildings to be emptied out during the rehab. In our minds, less is more, and we prefer the more conservative approach of adding value by enhancing curb appeal, upgrading the units, and addressing deferred maintenance.

Above all else, we want to ensure that each of the units is clean and safe for our tenants. This helps turn the apartments into stable communities, which helps us retain our tenants. Tenant retention helps reduce our expenses and in turn raise the excess cash flow from the investment.

Negotiating the Purchase Contract

We never go into a negotiation thinking that we need to sell the owner on our price. We prefer all involved parties walk away from a deal getting what they wanted, and that includes everyone from the seller to the broker. The concept of "win-win" drives everything we do, including negotiating the purchase of a property.

For example's sake, let us say that we found a promising property that needed to be put under contract right away. We start by taking all emotion out of the equation, and make it all about the numbers and nothing else. In an investment asset purchase, the numbers either work or they don't, and they never lie.

We must be willing to walk away from any and every deal if the numbers don't make sense; otherwise, we run the risk of overpaying for the property.

Our underwriting criteria set the price we're willing to pay, and we don't deviate from it. We have come to learn that great opportunities are not seen with our eyes, but rather with our minds, of which our underwriting and analysis is a product.

There are certain guidelines to which we strive to adhere when we go into a negotiation. First and most importantly, we try to have a positive attitude at all times. A successful deal is 90% mental, and a good attitude goes a long way toward mental clarity.

We also go above and beyond when it comes to preparation and research. Going into a negotiation knowing as much as we can about a property and its seller is crucial. By doing so, we have found that there is valuable information to be gained that can influence the structure of the deal.

For example, discovering that a seller has little or no debt against the property can influence the addition of an owner-carry note as part of the terms of our initial offer.

Next is our reputation. There is no way to buy a good reputation; you can only earn it. Above all else, what drives and defines our company is very simple: we are always completely ethical and we conduct our company and ourselves with the utmost integrity and professionalism, and we will never compromise on this.

In addition, we make a point to make doing business with The Capital 8 Group as easy as possible. This means maintaining a great service mentality, completing all transactions in as timely a manner as possible, and adhering to all deadlines.

Paying attention to details shows a seller that you are listening, builds confidence, and shows that you care about and value his time.

On the topic of listening, you simply must be a great listener if you are going to be successful. My dad taught me that you can't learn anything with your mouth open. Listening is a two-way street that involves being heard, and also hearing others' ideas, questions, and concerns. Oftentimes we will call a broker to discuss a particular property, and Shari will tell me to keep quiet and let him do the talking. And while it's always hard for me to stay quiet, I'll take her advice and listen as the broker tries to fill the silent spaces by divulging all sorts of valuable nuggets about the property, which are then stored away and become very useful in future negotiations.

I don't know that the importance of a sense of humor can be quantified. What I do know is that having one is essential to success in life and in business. Inevitably, there will be setbacks along the way, and learning to laugh about them serves to lift your spirit and dumbfounds the seller!

Lastly, remember that we are all human, and we all have good days and bad. On any given day, if there isn't a connection with a seller or a broker, try to remember that maybe their mind is elsewhere. Instead of becoming frustrated or disheartened, stop the conversation and ask if you could revisit it in a couple days. The seller or broker will likely be appreciative of the opportunity to relax and focus on whatever it is diverting his attention, and the subsequent chat is almost certain to go better.

Want a Steady Pay Raise?

By the time we close on a new property, we already have a plan in hand to raise the below market rental rates. Too many owners are afraid that if they raise rents, a few tenants might move out, thereby incurring the cost of turning the unit.

This fear is unjustified and unnecessary. Even in a down market, you can do a "nuisance increase", which entails increasing rents by $15-20 per month. The amount is not enough to compel tenants to move, as the cost to stay is far less than the cost of moving in terms of time, energy, and money. For most tenants, it's simply not worth the trouble to move over a $20 rent increase.

Multi-family building owners should be committed to continuously raising their rents in small increments. Between inflation, salaries, and cost of living, small increases to the rents are not only justified, but are expected by tenants. On a large scale, these small increases add up to significant numbers, which in turn increases not only the cash flow, but also the value of the property. This is one of the key characteristics of The Capital 8 Group. We continually strive to increase rents and drive the property value.

In a 100-unit building, a $20 per unit/month increase adds up to $24,000 per year. That is $24K in additional cash flow that can be distributed to investors or reinvested into the property. Not to mention that a $24K per year increase in cash flow translates to nearly $200K in increased value for the property. At one of our properties we increased the rent by as much as $175 per month, which when added up on an annual basis equates to a significant amount of money!

As a rule of thumb, always seek to increase your rents to market rate or just below. As long as you are treating your tenants well, they are expecting the increases and in most cases are happy to pay it knowing that you are providing them a clean, safe, and welcoming community in which to live.

Your Best Team Possible, Starting With the Broker

> *"Individual commitment to a group effort – that is what makes a team work, a company work, a society work, a civilization work." – Vince Lombardi*

One of the major building blocks of a successful company is creating the best team possible; a team that will ensure future success and take you to the finish line. This is exactly what The Capital 8 Group has done in each of the emerging markets we invest in. We have handpicked all of our team members based on their expertise in each of their specific fields. Their reputation and professionalism is a testament to our commitment to high standards of professionalism and excellence.

The commercial real estate broker is one of the most important members of our team. It is absolutely vital that we establish a relationship with an active, well-connected broker in each emerging market in which we invest. Brokers are a wealth of knowledge regarding the local market, and oftentimes they have access to listings that are not yet available to the general public. When a commercial broker gets a new listing, they immediately contact their short list of people with whom they have previously transacted business.

This strategy gives them the greatest possibility of double ending the commission on their deal, which of course, is their preference. Our goal is to work hard at creating relationships with top brokers so that we aren't only on their short list, but right at the top of it.

When we first started out it took us a little while to gain access to the best deals in a given market. We were certainly getting to look at properties, but they were what we'd consider to be the bottom of the barrel deals. Regular contact and coffee meetings with brokers wasn't helping us gain access to higher-quality deals, and we were stumped. A turning point came when we found out that one particular broker who was very active and well respected in the area was expecting a new baby with his wife.

We bought the couple a very nice baby gift for about $150, and we brought it to his office and gave it to him. It would be an understatement to say that the broker was surprised that someone he had barely known would be so thoughtful, and our $150 investment served to put us at the top of his thoughts. Just three days later, that same broker called and presented us with a great deal. We ended up putting that property under contract, 45 days later the broker had a million dollar sale, and we had our first property. Since that first purchase, we have bought over $10 million in properties through that broker, which began with a $150 baby gift. This simple gesture resulted in the act of reciprocity… of one person responding to a positive action with another positive action… and it has made this broker our go-to guy, and he has become a personal friend.

That is what we would consider an excellent return on investment!

A Real Estate Attorney on Your Team is a Must!

Just like many other professions, there are numerous areas of specialization for attorneys. You wouldn't see an ear doctor for a heart problem, so why would you have a general practice attorney handle the legal affairs of your real estate company? Doing so creates a significant, unnecessary risk for your company and your investors, and is a big mistake. In our mind, spending a little more money up-front for qualified legal help is well worth it considering that it may save tens of thousands of dollars in potential issues down the road.

In our company, we use at least two types of attorneys. The first type specializes only in real estate transactions, and understands the nuances, pitfalls, and risks involved with the purchase of such a large asset. When choosing a real estate attorney, it is important to use one that is licensed in the state in which you are investing, as there are many local variances that could significantly affect your deal if they were unknown to an out-of-state attorney.

The second type of lawyer we engage is a syndication attorney. We believe that dealing with other people's money is very serious business, and so does the Federal Government. The Securities & Exchange Commission has very specific rules that we all must follow, in addition to individual state laws that are equally complex. Engaging the services of a syndication attorney ensures that all legal documentation is clear, transparent, and compliant with all state and federal laws.

When choosing an attorney in a new market, we ask for referrals for attorneys, and we keep track of them. When a name pops up more than twice, we put that attorney on our interview list.

This strategy has worked out really well for us and as a result, we've built relationships with some excellent service providers. While this strategy requires a little more work up-front, when we are talking about such a crucial member of our team, it is well worth the extra effort.

Property Managers Are a Must on Your Team!

We all aren't experts at everything, and we believe that one of the smartest things a businessperson can do is to bring on good, quality people who are experts in their field. Filling a key role is our property manager. The manager is the person who handles the day-to-day operation of the property, deals with the tenants, collects the rent, and maintains the property. The list of functions this crucial person performs is endless, and we don't take his role lightly.

It is our practice to bring a property manager to any apartment we are considering purchasing because the more eyes on a property, the better. We ask them to prepare a "to do list" of items that need attention so that if we ultimately purchase the property we can immediately hit the ground running and begin our improvements the day the transaction closes. This goes a long way toward showing our tenants that we care about them, and the property, and that we intend to bring positive change to the property and their lives.

When dealing with a property management company, there are red flags that indicate that they may not be doing their job. One of the most obvious ones is a dramatic increase in Notices to Vacate. If more than a few tenants are submitting their notices, it is an indication that many more tenants are probably unhappy. Generally speaking, unhappy tenants are slower to pay rent and less likely to renew their leases.

Another red flag is higher than average vacancy rates. Correcting this issue is simple, and the fastest way is to ask the property manager for a copy of the traffic report and the conversion rates. Simply asking for that information is usually enough to compel the property manager to give your property some increased focus, which can quickly solve the problem.

A costly red flag is when the management company takes too long to complete the turns on recently vacated units. Under no circumstance should a turn take more than 3-5 days, and exceeding that amount of time is simply unacceptable. Doing so can quickly and severely affect your cash flow and vacancy rate.

Other red flags include collection issues, deferred maintenance, and being charged for repairs that were never completed. If a tenant's rent is late, it is incumbent on the property manager to immediately get in contact with the tenant and remind him that payment is due.

Deferred maintenance indicates an inattentive property manager. Discovering that you were billed for work that was never completed could be something as simple as an error in the property manager's accounting records, or as serious as revealing a problem with his integrity.

Once you do find a great property manager, treat that person like gold! Show them you appreciate what they do by giving them gifts and remembering important days in their lives. Make sure you give them the authority to maintain your property and keep it clean and safe. Tell them where they can improve and where they are exceeding your expectations. Once you understand the value of a quality property manager, you'll want to do whatever you can to keep them around.

Commercial Insurance Agent Team Member

Good insurance agents not only make sure you are properly indemnified from risks, but they also keep you updated on changes that affect your property and policy. Two of the biggest mistakes investors make are to go with the least expensive insurance quotes and not taking the time to fully understand the various types of coverage and their corresponding limits.

Some agents will knowingly quote an inferior policy in order to come in as the least expensive option and win the policy on price alone. Having an agent who understands the potential risks, local laws, and types of insurance available may be one of the best decisions you ever make as an apartment owner.

In some jurisdictions, an event like a fire in one individual unit of an apartment complex will trigger a requirement that the entire building, and not just the damaged unit, be brought up to current code standards. If an owner has an inferior insurance policy that doesn't cover such an event, this could be an extremely expensive oversight. In addition, there are lost rents due to units being out of commission during rehabilitation, costs involved with certain types of remediation, and many other pitfalls that are completely avoidable with a little extra planning on the front end.

The bottom line is that it is never a good idea to cut corners when it comes to selecting a good insurance agent. The best thing to do is to find somebody who above all has your best interests in mind.

A Great CPA is an Absolute Must!

The CPA is often an overlooked member of the team, but in our opinion one of the most valuable and important roles to be filled. Finding a well-educated CPA that loves what he does and who specializes in real estate companies is a crucial task, and is one that needs to be taken very seriously. Your CPA should be responsible for maintaining the books, preparing annual tax returns, and ideally providing advice on topics like cash flow, budgets, tax planning, and anything else pertaining to the financial operation of your properties.

A Commercial Appraiser on Your Team is a Bonus!

We fully understood the value of a commercial real estate appraiser as a team member when we owned a few properties and one particular appraiser would call us and talk at length about our rents, price per square foot, how we were improving the property, and what we were seeing in the market. We knew that if he was asking detailed questions about our properties, then he was surely asking those same questions about others in the area.

As a result, we knew he was a source of information on the overall market and the details behind it. Not only would his advice be invaluable as it pertained to the properties we already owned, but he could also provide invaluable insight about properties we were considering buying. Don't overlook the value of having access to one or several good, highly qualified appraisers in the various markets in which you invest.

Loan Servicer – You Gotta Love 'Em!

We always strive to underwrite properties as accurately as possible and with the timeliest information, we can attain. In order to do that, we have on our team an incredibly responsive loan servicer who keeps us up to date with interest rates, loan terms, outlooks, and so on. This person is very in-tune with the financial markets, and he calls us regularly with updates.

Without him on our team, we would likely end up paying more than we have to in financing costs.

Big Mistakes Investors Make

At the top of our list of potential mistakes is thinking that one person can do it all. Once our entire team was established, we quickly noticed that our workload and stress level was significantly reduced. As a result of lower stress and workload, we were happier, more efficient, and even looked more professional! We loved that we could pick up the phone, call any member of our team of professionals, and almost immediately get the answers we needed.

We can remember a particular instance where we were in negotiations on a property. Hoping that we could glean some valuable information, we called our property manager to get his opinion on something. It turned out that he had already walked this particular property and had knowledge of some major drainage and sewer issues in addition to other problems that had simply been "covered up". That five minute phone call ended up saving us a lot of time and money, once again proving just how valuable having great team members is to us.

Another mistake commonly made by investors is thinking that any investment is a good investment. Almost daily, we receive offering memorandums pitching a property and talking about how great of an investment it would be. We may even pick up the phone and call the broker, who inevitably will say that we need to move quickly and jump on this once-in-a-lifetime investment opportunity.

When this happens, just keep in mind that most of the time the broker's opinion and comments are influenced at some level by their commission check. It is not up to the broker to decide if a property is a suitable investment; it is up to us. We have trained ourselves to be unemotional when analyzing a property. In the end, if the numbers work then we move forward. If they don't work, we move on.

Investing in a market that is approaching the end of the recovery phase is another mistake. At this point, prices are already elevated and we don't like to be late to the party. Instead, we like to purchase our properties before the news coverage and general consensus reveals that the particular market has recovered and is seeing increased values. Early on in the recovery phase, there is less competition and the pricing is much better. Don't make the mistake of entering a market too late.

Ignoring overbuilding in the area surrounding your properties is a very costly and stressful mistake. We understand that if we own a C-property in a neighborhood of newly built A-properties, the operation of our apartment complex will be negatively impacted despite the fact that they are completely different classes of properties. We can expect to see aggressive move-in specials at the new complex that are designed to drive rapid tenant acquisition.

This directly affects our building by changing the expectations of the potential tenant. If she is comparing what she can get with our C-property to what she can get for only slightly more monthly rent at the new A-property because of its aggressive move-in specials, the chances are pretty high that we will lose her business.

All of this is to say that we look hard for barriers to entry when purchasing multi-family properties. These barriers can be natural or man-made, and they are important. Recently when we purchased a property in the metro Denver area, we found out during our due diligence that the city government did not want to permit the construction of any new apartment buildings within city limits. This served as a strong man-made barrier to entry that minimized our potential future competition.

It should go without saying, but overpaying for a property is a deadly, albeit common mistake. We never use someone else's underwriting, especially if it is the broker's. It is not uncommon for a broker to accidentally leave out key expenses such as taxes, insurance, or financing costs. From our perspective, a cost is a cost, and they all affect the cash-on-cash returns we are getting. Every expense counts and every expense should be counted.

Forgetting expenses when underwriting a property most often results in overpaying for the property.

Lurking beneath the surface of a property is a mistake that could cost you dearly. I'm talking about environmental risks. When we purchase a property, we always order a Phase One environmental inspection and make the purchase subject to a satisfactory report. This thorough report determines if there are any unseen environmental hazards on your property. These risks include underground storage tanks, seepage, hazardous chemicals, asbestos, and other potentially expensive sources of pollution.

The costs of environmental hazard remediation can be astronomical, and the burden to bear such costs falls on the owner. Think of obtaining an environmental report as an additional layer of insurance, as its cost is nothing compared to the costs of cleaning up a hazard that you could have avoided had you only done your homework.

Lastly, prior to purchasing a property it is important to physically walk into and inspect each and every unit. Not doing so could be an enormous mistake, as there is a good chance that the only units you will be shown by brokers or sellers are those without the deadbeat tenants, hoarders, or those without major defects or deferred maintenance. Inspecting every unit prior to closing is your one and only chance to be compensated for anything that is wrong with the property that would otherwise go unnoticed. This is also a great time to create a list of comments for each unit that spells out the issues that need to be addressed immediately upon taking over the property.

As a matter of practice, Shari and I go into every single apartment unit, and usually with our inspector. Well, I go into every single apartment unit, and Shari goes into *most* of them. If she sees a filthy unit, or one with a pit bull, she opts to stay outside and wait while I go inspect the unit. She figures there is no point in both of us being subjected to whatever it is that is inside the unit!

Take Action

"Life is won by those who take action." – David Lindahl

Successful people do two things that unsuccessful people tend not to do. First, they strive to continually educate themselves, and secondly when it's time to take action, they do. By reading this chapter, you are already demonstrating a commitment to educating yourself and making a better life for you and your family. If you've read even just a portion of this chapter, you are most likely fascinated by the prospect of creating significant wealth by investing in apartments. It is my hope that you have gained an understanding of what our company does and how we do it.

Now it is time to take action! Don't let your enthusiasm grow stale. Instead, keep progressing toward your goal of financial freedom.

Think about the joy and fulfillment you will feel when explaining to your family and friends that you own part of one or more apartment buildings. Imagine the satisfaction you'll experience every time you receive a monthly distribution check, or a huge payout from the sale of a building, knowing that you are taking action to secure your family's future.

You have an amazing life in front of you! No matter where you've been, who you are, or what you've done up to this point, today is the beginning of the rest of your life. You were born to live an incredible life that is filled with promise and potential. Don't stop dreaming. Don't accept the lie that dreams and reality cannot co-exist. Remember that those without dreams fail to inspire the success stories that we long to hear. You have permission to dream, and to dream big!

<u>About Us</u>

    We are Jeff and Shari Kissee, Co-Founders and Principals of **The Capital 8 Group**, a Denver-based commercial real estate investment company.

    We are family-oriented individuals with a laser focus on creating wealth and preserving time for our family, friends, and community. Our passion is showing others that it is possible to live a better, lower-stress, more fulfilling life than they ever thought possible. Through the business model of **The Capital 8 Group**, our desires have become reality.

    Since our companies beginning, we have invested in numerous commercial properties including multi-family, retail, and self-storage.

    Our combined education and experience in business, commercial real estate development and management, accounting, construction, architecture, and engineering dovetails nicely with our business model. We continue to actively buy and sell properties in emerging markets across the United States, all to the benefit of our investors and ourselves.

We are committed to always furthering our education, surrounding ourselves with the right team of mentors and professionals, and doing everything with the utmost integrity, service, and excellence.

So what does this all mean? How do you go about taking the first step and get started in real estate investing? If you've read this chapter, you're already well along your way. While we are not saying that investing with **The Capital 8 Group** is the only way to get ahead in real estate, we are certain that our business model and company is the best way.

Make the decision now to change the trajectory of your life. Follow the advice of Robert Frost, and take the road less traveled. It will make all the difference.

Pick up the phone and connect with us, send an email or visit us online at www.Capital8group.com. If we can't help you achieve your dreams, then we are committed to helping you figure out who can. Our promise to you is that it will be the best, most meaningful phone call you have ever made.

Jeff and Shari Kissee
The Capital 8 Group, LLC
3845 Tennyson Street, Ste. 107
Denver, CO 80212
(303) 940-1220

ANALYZING COMMERCIAL REAL ESTATE FOR MAXIMUM PROFITS

Greg Johnston

BE THE CONDUCTOR OF YOUR FINANCIAL SUCCESS

ANALYZE THE DEAL

If you watch a professional football game, you see the coach does not do too much on the sidelines. He knew what he was going to do before the first play was ever executed. He knows his players inside and out, he knows their strengths and their weaknesses. He has scouted the opposing team and has studied the predicted outcome of different formations and player match ups. The coach has gone over defensive and offensive schemes with his assistant coaches and players. The coach is staking the odds of success in his favor. The coach is the conductor of his team. He has determined his success before stepping on the field.

As the conductor of your commercial real estate investments, you need to immerse yourself into the details to analyze the strengths and weaknesses of potential deals. Investing in commercial real estate, without understanding the numbers, is no different than leading a football team without doing the preparations to ensure your success. This chapter will cover the necessary equations to quickly analyze a potential investment property. More importantly this chapter will explain what those numbers mean to you and to your potential investment.

It is easy to become overwhelmed when looking at financials. While evaluating commercial real estate, you may not truly understand the numbers behind the deal. You start feeling overwhelmed, your eyes glaze over and you begin just to skim over pertinent information instead of actually comprehending it. It is vital to know which numbers you need to obtain, and to understand what those numbers mean to your investment.

Beginners often find it daunting to wade through all the financial statements involved in analyzing a deal. It is not enough to just know the formulas you also need to understand what the results mean. This chapter will take you through the essential math to quickly and confidently analyze any potential investment property. After completing this chapter, you will be able to break down the formulas needed to understand what the results mean to your deal.

I like the math. The numbers tell you the true story of a potential investment. They will tell you if the property is making or losing money very quickly. If I were to do a "deep dive" analysis into every deal I looked at, there would be time for little else. The math discussed in this chapter will qualify whether the investment is valid for the next step of the analysis.

There are three calculations that need to be performed before a property can pass my initial go-no-go evaluation. These three indicators are the capitalization rate, debt coverage ratio and the cash on cash return. If the results from these calculations are within my accepted range, this would be a deal I would take to the next level of due diligence. We need to take a look at each of these indicators in depth:

CAP RATE

The Capitalization Rate, also known as the cap rate, is a rate of return on real estate investment property based on the expected income that the property will generate. The cap rate is used to estimate the investor's potential return on his or her investment. But what does the number mean and how can we use it to analyze our deals?

First, we need to understand a few fundamental terms and how they are calculated. The EGI, or Effective Gross Income, is the amount of income produced by a property, plus miscellaneous income, less vacancy costs and collection losses. The miscellaneous income could be late fees, pet premium fees, laundry facility fees, on-site storage unit fees.

Effective Gross Income (EGI) = Income - Collection Losses

Look at an example of an apartment complex that has an income of $250,000 if every unit were rented out. The rent roll shows the apartment complex typically renting 80% of its units. 20% of the units are not rented which means you are unable to collect $50,000 ($250,000 * 0.2). The EGI for the property is:

$$EGI = 250,000 - 50,000 = \$200,000$$

You also need to know how to calculate Operating Expenses and Capital Expenses. Operating expenses are what a business incurs as a result of performing its normal, everyday business operations: employee wages, utility costs, lawn maintenance, snow removal, housekeeping, insurance, taxes are all considered operating expenses. Capital expenses, sometimes referred to as a Below-the-Line cost, is an expense that does not occur in the property's day-to-day operations. In other words, they are not commonly repeated. These can include replacing the roof, new carpet, replacing a boiler or air conditioner.

Net Operating Income (NOI) The NOI is the annual income generated by a property after taking into account all income collected from operations, and deducting all expenses incurred from operations. As a formula, it would look like:

Net Operating Income = Effective Gross Income · Net Operating Expenses

The NOI is essential to understanding commercial real estate investments. If the NOI is positive, then the operating income exceeds the gross operating expenses. If the NOI is negative, then the operating expenses exceeds the gross operating income. The NOI can either be based on historical financial data or on forward-looking estimates called pro forma. You always want your financial due diligence based on actual historical data. Pro forma numbers will be discussed in more detail later. The NOI measures a property's ability to produce an income stream.

That brings us back to cap rate. The cap rate is the ratio between the net operating income produced by the asset and its capital cost.

$$\textbf{Cap Rate} = \frac{\textbf{Net Operating Income (NOI)}}{\textbf{Cost (or value)}}$$

For example, a property was presented to me with a purchase price of \$2,800,000. After doing my financial due diligence I have determined the NOI to be \$277,197. If we plug that into our formula, it will look like this:

$$\text{Cap Rate} = \frac{277,197}{2,800,000} = 0.09899 \ (*100) = 9.89 \text{ or } 9.9\%$$

On this particular deal I have a cap rate of 9.9%. However, what does it mean to have a 9.9% cap rate?

The cap rate shows the potential rate of return on the real estate investment for one year assuming the property was bought as an all cash deal. The other factor you should consider when looking at the cap rate is the class of property you are considering. Commercial properties can be designated into four separate classes; they are either an A, B, C or D class property. With a class A property being a new construction, not more than ten years old, to a class D property that is typically 30 years and older and in a "war zone" area. You can find more detailed information about property class and neighborhood class on my Web site at www.RealEstateDealAnalyzer.com/class.

For this class of property, I am typically looking for a minimum of an 8% cap rate. So a cap rate of 9.9% is above my acceptable threshold.

Many times, when you are looking at analyzing a commercial deal, brokers will not give you a sale price. Instead, they will only tell you the property is going for Market Value. If you have a good relationship with that broker, he may give you some indication as to what the seller is looking to get for his property. Without that information, you can figure out what an acceptable offer price could be by manipulating the cap rate formula like this:

$$\text{Value} = \frac{\text{NOI}}{\text{Cap Rate}}$$

We know the NOI to be $277,197, and we know we are looking for at lease a cap rate of 8%. Plug those numbers into the formula and we get:

$$\text{Value} = \frac{277,197}{0.08} = 3,464,962$$

In negotiating our purchase price, we know that to get a cap rate of 8% we cannot pay more than $3,500,000. Anything more than that would bring our cap rate lower than 8% and any price less than $3,500,000 will give us a greater cap rate.

CASH ON CASH RETURN

Another crucial indicator is the Cash On Cash return. This indicator is a simple measure of investment performance that tells us how fast we will get our money back. By dividing your annual cash flow (before taxes) by your acquisition costs, you will come up with your cash on cash return.

The acquisition cost is the total of what you put down to purchase the property including the down payment and any other initial expenses. The annual cash flow is nothing more than the NOI less the Debt Service, with the debt service being how much money is owed on a loan, including both the interest and the principal amounts.

$$\text{Cash on Cash Return} = \frac{\text{Annual Before Tax Cash Flow}}{\text{Total Cash Invested}} = \frac{\text{NOI - Debt Service}}{\text{Acquisition Costs}}$$

Going back to the example of our $2,800,000 property: when all of the acquisition costs are totaled up, we need

$733,600 to purchase this property. The annual cash flow before taxes is $89,946. Our formula will look like:

$$\textbf{Cash on Cash Return} = \frac{89,946}{733,600} = 0.1226 \ (*100) = 12.3\%$$

Based on the figures above, the cash on cash return told me the year one return on investment would be 12.3%. Considering I look for a 12% or better cash on cash return, this property was looking more promising with each calculation. One more benchmark calculation required to see if this if this property warrants further investigation is the Debt Coverage Ratio.

DEBT COVERAGE RATIO

Debt Coverage Ratio, also referred to as Debt Service Coverage Ratio (DSCR), is a financial ratio that indicates whether or not your property is generating enough income to cover its debt. The debt coverage ratio compares the property's net operating income with its total debt service obligations. This indicator is a useful benchmark that shows the financial strength of the property.

A debt coverage ratio of 1.0 means the property is generating just enough income to pay back its loan. Anything less than 1.0 would show a negative cash flow. If you have a debt coverage ratio of 0.9. That would mean there is only enough net operating income to cover 90% of the annual debt payments. In other words, the property is not producing enough money to cover the mortgage. The formula looks like:

$$\textbf{Debt Coverage Ratio} = \frac{\textbf{NOI}}{\textbf{Debt Service}}$$

I like to see a conservative debt coverage ratio of at least 1.6 or better. That means for every dollar of mortgage payment I need to make, I will have $1.60 coming in. A lender typically likes to see a debt coverage ratio of 1.2 or better. The higher the ratio, the easier it will be to obtain a loan. I like to have a bigger buffer for unknowns that can creep in after properties are purchased.

Using the $2,800,000 property example the formula would equate to:

$$\textbf{Debt Coverage Ratio} = \frac{263,697}{136,819} = 1.93$$

NOTE: You will see that the NOI in this example is $13,500 less than the NOI example I showed calculating the Cap Rate. That is because in calculating the debt coverage ratio I subtracted the capital expenses from the NOI. Again, I like to be conservative in my calculations. I would rather under commit and over perform.

This example property has a debt coverage ratio of 1.93. For every dollar of mortgage payment that will need to be made, we will have $1.93 coming in. This benchmark illustrates this property to be a reasonably safe deal.

NAPKIN TEST

Taking a look at a quick napkin test, we need to determine if the asset we have been using as an example qualifies for further review and analysis.

The minimum we are looking for:

Cap Rate = 8%+
Cash on Cash Return = 12%+
Debt Coverage Ratio = 1.6%+

Our calculations show:

Cap Rate = 9.9%
Cash on Cash Return = 12.3%
Debt Coverage Ratio = 1.9%

Based on the calculations we have covered in this chapter, at a purchase price of $2,800,000, this is a property that would pique my interest. This property is worth a further, deeper analysis. I would have a letter of intent submitted to the selling broker, and if accepted, I would complete a full due diligence package on this property.

THE NEXT STEP

A good deal will not be on the open market long. Even if a broker is giving you a pocket listing you will need to move on these deals in less than 24 hours, preferably the same day it is given to you. A broker will not keep a good deal quiet for a very long. That does not necessarily mean you have to submit a "Letter of Intent" (LOI) that day. At the very least, you need to let your broker know whether or not you are interested in pursuing the presented property.

It is crucial to your broker relationship that you provide an answer as soon as possible. Even if the numbers are not what you are looking for, it is important to let them know immediately why this deal does not work for you and exactly what you are looking for, be very specific. When Your broker trusts that you will consistently get back to him quickly, he will begin funneling more deals your way that are better aligned with your requirements.

PRO FORMA

The pro forma describes a method of tackling financial results in order to emphasize either current or projected figures. The pro forma is an assumed, forecasted financial statement generated to give you an idea of how the actual statement will look if the underlying assumptions hold true. In other words, it is the best guess estimate of the projected cash flow. It is important to look at historical data.

At minimum, you want to see the monthly detailed numbers, known as the "trailing 12." If it is available, two years of the trailing 12 is preferable. You will want to see the trailing 12 for the profit and loss statements and also looking at past and current rent rolls. The P&L statements will give you the details of how the property is performing.

Anyone handing you a pro forma package of a property is in essence giving you a work of fiction. You never base your financial due diligence on pro forma numbers. That is so important it is worth repeating: never base your financial analysis off of the numbers found on a pro forma statement. You want to look at the actual, historical and current numbers as the basis of your financial analysis.

Sometimes it is going to be easy to read the financials. In many cases, you are going to be dealing with mom-and-pop owners that have been managing the property themselves. If you are purchasing a self-managed property, the financials may be so difficult to wade through, you may be tempted to use pro forma numbers to get your results. I once had an owner fax me several handwritten pages that looked like he generated them just to fax them to me. There was nothing historical, nothing detailed, just a bunch of handwritten statements.

I am not saying to ignore these, they may turn out to be a superb deal. In a case like this, you just have to dig deeper. You need to keep asking questions, asking for actual figures, receipts, bank statements, tax returns, whatever it takes for you to feel confident you know exactly what is going on with the property.

Pro forma statements are based on a rosy future. If all the assumptions the broker or the seller are stating actually happens, then the pro forma statement numbers may come true. But what if they do not? What if the market does not perform as the pro forma suggests, or a natural disaster happens in the area? Any number of things that could potentially affect the property. At that point, speculative assumptions go out the window.

Recently, I had an investor email me the details of a property he wanted to partner on. The trailing 12 was a one-sheet summary. That summary did not tell me anything about what is going on with the property. There were some rather large differences year-over-year for the last few years. Without the details, I do not know why the differences are occurring. You will be able to see, on a monthly basis, where the money is being spent and where the money is coming from.

I was analyzing a different property that had a category of "other income" with about $5,000 showing up every month. It took me several requests to the broker to show me where the income was coming from. Eventually, I found that it was funds the seller was pumping into the property from his personal account to make the numbers look better than they were. False income distorts all other figures.

One mistake I have seen newer investors make is to skim over the numbers without really understanding what they are looking at. Do not just assume anything, ask questions and get satisfactory answers, answers that make sense to you.

BONUS

I hope this chapter has helped you understand the necessary math to pre-qualify a potential investment. As you are developing relationships with your brokers, and they ask you what kind of numbers you are looking for, you will be able to tell them with confidence what you want to see in a property. You will be confident that it is not just a number that you are throwing out. You will now have an understanding of what those numbers mean to a property's performance.

As mentioned before, it is paramount to respond to brokers quickly. It is just as vital to be able to present your data to potential investors. This is done through a detailed property package.

I have developed a Web site at RealEstateDealAnalyzer.com that will help you calculate all the math needed to analyze your commercial investment, including what has been covered in this chapter. My site will also provide you with information that can be used in your property package. Information that every investor will want to see, like: equity return at resale, projected owner cash flow, acquisition expenses, loan information and much more.

When I first started in this business, I was lost on how to create a property package that would entice potential investors. I was fortunate enough to befriend fellow real estate entrepreneurs who were willing to share their property packages with me. I pulled the "best of" from these packages and have created a comprehensive presentation package.

It takes time and effort to re-create a new property package for every deal you are pursuing. I automated the process making it easier for myself. I have taken that information and created this Web site.

By filling in some basic information this Web site will generate the core financial data needed to populate your property package. I have included an example of a completed package on the site. You will need to generate the narrative. This example will help guide you in creating the narrative and the layout. I thank you in advance for visiting my Web site RealEstateDealAnalyzer.com and I hope you find it useful.

HOW TO BE MENTORED

Diane Bowman

I ve been a real estate mentor for over ten years now and I am often asked, "how does that work?" No two mentorships should be exactly the same for any mentor or participant. The idea of a mentorship should be to take the participant from where they are today to the next level.

That being said I would like to share a few stories that may help you better prepare to receive the information provided by those you choose to follow.

It is easier to absorb water with a sponge than with brick.

Both of these items are porous but the sponge will soak up anything and everything while the brick just gets damp. If you are hard and rigid in your thinking or have your own idea of what it takes to be like the mentor you may never hear what the mentor is really saying.

By example while working with two business owners I was discussing our corporate structures for our securities transactions. I had explained why we use two entities and the operating agreements that our Security Attorneys prepare. We carried on a back and forth discussion for several hours about previous transactions, investor relations, protective clauses, voting rights, you name it.

This discussion was very in depth and contained multiple scenarios. Both of the business owners followed easily and asked great questions. Every so often during the discussion Partner One would go back as to why we set up two companies for each purchase. I would stop and go back through the entire setup again trying new terminology to explain the same process.

This went on several times during the course of about four hours. As we were preparing to move to the next phase of the mentorship Partner One once again stopped to say I had never yet explained why we used two companies, and he just could not move forward until I did.

It became clear that Partner Two was tired of hearing this and wanted to move on, but also did not want to try and explain it on his own. Finally, Partner One stated that during a break he had called his attorney and the attorney stated there were ways to set up the deal using only one entity. I agreed and stated that we were doing it for financial reasons not legal reasons. The structure I described allowed the business owners to partner with a high net worth individual to secure financing for larger deals.

Partner One was embarrassed and admitted that he had heard me say that at the beginning of the discussion and multiple times throughout that the entity was used to secure financing.

This person's brick wall was in assuming that anything to do with entity structure was purely for asset protection purposes, when in fact all your entities should be reviewed for legal, tax, and financial impact. The ironic part of this is the reason for their mentorship was to assist them with securing financing.

Respect your mentor but don't revere them.

Mentors are simply people with skills or experience that can shorten your learning curve.

Very often participants will engage a mentor to assist in improving some aspect of the participant's life. The mentor usually has a wealth of knowledge and experience to share in that aspect, for instance sports, nutrition, health, real estate, stocks, business etc. The Participant can't wait to tap into that knowledge.

Somewhere between the initial engagement of a mentor and the actual interaction. Participants develop an idea that the Mentor must be perfect. I have seen this sabotage many a mentorship because the Participant finds fault with a certain aspect of the Mentor and therefore discounts the value of the knowledge.

I was fortunate enough during my years of employment to work for several first generation millionaires. All of these gentlemen had knowledge and skills that were invaluable to my professional growth, but I never imagined for a moment that any of them were perfect.

One person had one of the most creative business minds I have ever met. However, that creative mind could not match clothes. He did not dress the part and on some days could be mistaken for a maintenance man.

Another individual built a few businesses from scratch and was a mastermind at creating business partnerships. He was and continues to be a prime example of a true business leader. As the Businessman, he made sure to match the right expertise partners with the right idea and the right financing to make the project a success. From a personal standpoint he was also an expert at divorce without prenuptial agreements.

Had I discounted his business knowledge because of his personal life I would have missed many opportunities along the way.

I have had participants tell me they knew I was "good" because of the kind of shoes I wore, and others tell me that I must not be good because I fly coach unless I can get a free or discounted upgrade.

One of my peers received a bad review because he did not eat Sushi.

None of that matters! Don't judge just learn!

Remember, when working with your mentor respect their knowledge and guidance. They know what it takes to be successful in their field.

I recently had dinner with a very successful couple whom were mentored a few years ago. Since beginning to recognize their dreams, they have been asked several times why they feel they have succeeded so much more than many others who received the same education.

The answers are very similar to my own story.

1. Be Honest - A good mentor is there to help you achieve the next level of your success. We do not care where you live, the kind of car you drive, or even where we may eat together. The more honest you are with the mentor about your history, current financial position, and goals the more successful the mentorship will be.

I have had a few examples that will help you to better

understand the importance of this rule. I was mentoring a couple on the West Coast. We were working on finding, rehabbing, and reselling working class homes. The participants were in their early fifties and one had a slight disability. Even though I asked multiple times about their current financial position, they always skirted the question.

We worked together for three long days and put together a solid plan of action for finding investment areas, analyzing properties, and hiring contractors. We were even able to get the first property under contract. I was struggling to assist them with securing financing because I had no idea of their financial position.

I was helping them to interview hard money lenders for the purchase and rehab because I assumed they had no cash or credit. After the second phone call the gentlemen said, "I guess we should tell you that we are multi-millionaires and won't need hard money, but I would really like to know how that works".

We are now in the last hours of the last day and all I can do is introduce the concepts. Had the couple been honest up front I would have structured the mentorship so they could put their cash and net worth to work.

While they were very pleased with all we accomplished they readily admitted that our time together would have been better spent in another direction.

For this couple it was just a matter of purchasing a second mentorship, but for many that is not an option so please use your time wisely.

2. Communicate with the Mentor on the Mentor's terms.

If the Mentor prefers phone calls to emails or texts, that is how you communicate. If you are asking for help or assistance you will get the best information if the Mentor is comfortable with the exchange.

In my case I prefer an email if the question is more than one or two lines long, if shorter a text is fine. I prefer this because I travel quite a bit and have my own businesses to run. I can't always answer the phone.

This method also allows me to think about the question and in some cases tap into my resources for possible suggestions.

3. Do what the Mentor says.

These students attribute their success to doing exactly what their Mentors said. Even though on many occasions they were pushed outside their comfort zone they did it anyway.

The result was very often they were amazed that the method actually worked.

I am living proof of this last bit of advice. Believe it or not my greatest fear was talking to strangers. My husband Bob and I engaged with a mentor to help us create our own real estate business.

Bob was a business machine sales manager and I had many years of experience working in the real estate industry, but it was always working for others.

Our mentor Margie came in to town and really

challenged our comfort zones. We were both managers in our positions and now we are putting out hand written signs that say, "Bob Buys Houses" and she wanted us to put the magnets on our car! Oh the shame of it all.

She was only here for three days, we will just go along, and how bad can it be. Well much to our surprise people actually began calling. Bob was great on the phone and also in person when talking to potential sellers and power team members. I was in the background taking notes and reminding Bob of things I needed to know. For the first day and a half I did all I could to stay in the car and avoid meetings of any kind. Bob was clearly carrying the burden.

Margie was having no part of this. She pretended her leg hurt and jumped in the back seat of the minivan behind Bob. I sat in the back passenger seat because I felt no one would make me get out and talk from back there. Boy was I wrong.

We spotted a potential property and I told Bob to go talk to the guy. He of course told me to do it. Margie said forget it she will go, so I opened the door and stepped out to let her out. As I was stepping out she put her foot on my behind and gave a little shove, when I was clear of the door she shut and locked it.

They left me standing on the sidewalk. I felt I would look worse pounding on the van door than walking up and talking to the man so I went and inquired about the property. I GOT IT UNDER CONTRACT!!

As the story goes that kick in the behind changed my life. We have been totally reliant on our real estate business for over 10 years, through good and bad real estate times.

I attribute all of our success to the many mentors and trainers that provided us with insight and education, most often 3 Days at a time through weekend seminars.

I am now a Mentor and multi-award winning International Commercial Real Estate Speaker.

Feel free to contact this author at A3daystowealth@aol.com

You may also look forward soon to our website: 3DaystoWealth.com

Diane Bowman
Commercial Real Estate Elite Trainer
Real Estate Public Speaker
Mentor

The 5 Keys to Finding Your Ideal Business Partner:
The Mach 5 Real Estate Story

The 5 Keys to Finding Your Ideal Business Partner:

The Mach 5 Real Estate Story

KEY #1: "All by myself" is a fool's trap! Consider the logic of partnering.

Even though "right now is the best time to enter multifamily investing," according to Forbes Magazine, many people try to do it all themselves. I see this same dangerous trap happen time and time again. Many well intentioned people become overwhelmed when trying to make their financial goals happen alone.

Let's all face it, we have all done this… your brain wanders off and sees yourself wearing the real estate super hero cape, standing tall. You did it, all by yourself! 100% of the deal is yours. The daydream fades, you look down at a to-do list with the 42 steps in a single multifamily deal. In haste, you find someone at a local meeting feeling the same and join forces… for a while. That is the typical broken approach the majority take to investing. What if you could learn how to avoid the trap of either going solo or haphazardly partnering?

The reality is the business of multifamily is a team sport, based on developing long term relationships with highly competent people. A partner can be a fantastic opportunity, particularly if you take the effort to define and select the right person that can drive your goals to the next level. Instead of a haphazard method of finding this person, you will leave this chapter knowing EXACTLY how to get the right partner into your business venture.

My name is Joe Milunas, co-owner of Mach 5 Real Estate. Our company specializes in providing apartment investment opportunities to people just like you who want both cash flow and appreciation, yet don't want to work 70 hour weeks doing it yourself. We are conservative investors and our vision is simple. We provide our clients access to fantastic, managed-for-you apartment deals that are usually only accessible to large, institutional investors.

In order to accomplish this big vision, I knew that I would need a world class leader to join me. Investors do not want a solo team leader, they prefer the security of knowing the organization, regardless of size has at least two key leaders.

The right person would not just double our combined results, but a true synergy would act as an exponential multiplier. Let me show you how this vision became a reality.

Meet David Harrison, Mach 5 Real Estate's Co-Owner

My business partner, David Harrison, is a knockout expense reduction specialist and entrepreneur. In fact, he is number 1 in the country for most units under his expense reduction program. Before joining forces, David Harrison had accumulated 125,000 units inside of his Nationwide Green Consultants expense reduction service. It continues to rapidly grow and currently has 131,264 units. Not only that, David has completed over 125 million in multifamily real estate deals as a broker at Sperry Van Ness dating back to 2000.

David's background was a key influence on my careful selection of him to join Mach 5 Real Estate. Once I defined exactly what Mach 5 needed to grow exponentially, I wanted a business partner with access to hidden deals. Inside of his expense reduction client relationships are a massive vein of untapped gold: off market deals. David is often first to learn when the owner wants to sell. This unique factor allows us to get better pricing, better deals, and beat the pants off the competition.

The investors that we carefully select to join our deals not only have my extensive experience in increasing occupancy, but David's ability to reduce expenses. This partnership is an outstanding synergy, but it did not happen by accident. In the sections that follow, you will learn the precise process I used to define and locate such an ideal business partner.

Where I learned to do this was in business graduate school at the ripe age of 34. Instead of suggesting you spend two years doing what I did, simply pay attention and I will teach you exactly how to select partners to achieve your goals.

Master's Degree: How to Build Teams

I have been able to generate some serious success in real estate and business working by myself. It did become clear into my career, that to do large multifamily, I would need a team of outstanding people. Realizing the importance attracting exceptional talent, I actually decided to specialize in the area of building world class teams.

I was recruited by one of the best business programs in the Midwest and completed a Master's of Science in Organizational Management. During these two intense years, using the same method as Harvard Business School, at Chadron we analyzed business successes and failures through in depth case studies and internships. One key element was apparent, the selection of the right leadership team is imperative to turn any service or product into a winning business.

"Generating outstanding results is about knowing exactly which people are required to exceed the client's needs."

Joe Milunas, PMP, MSOM
Author & Multifamily Entrepreneur

KEY #2: Build your brand and core values first, then select your partner.

Knowing your core values can set you apart in the crowded real estate marketplace. In 2004, I co-founded North San Diego Real Estate Investors. The first meeting had 25 attendees. I built the key marketing systems and joint ventures to make the group attendance explode to over 200 within 16 months.

More so than these systems, I successfully designed a service that did not exist in the area. Yes there were other real estate clubs in San Diego, but our model of round tables with member to member interaction set us apart. This was one of my first successes of clearly defining a core value "member interaction" for example, and hitting it.

By leading this real estate club for three years, I got to see the industry in depth. As much as we wanted our members to take action, they were bombarded with a different investment strategy each month. I quickly realized that many club members end up never taking any action. This is not due to a lack of education or even capital surprisingly. The answer would surprise you.

The inaction is caused by confusion, the fear they are not doing the right thing. With this problem in the marketplace, I decided to create a company and vision to meet the needs of this group, by providing world class, passive investments. In order to accomplish this, I needed two things. First, I needed a unique business strategy and brand that instilled confidence.

Second, I needed a world class real estate mentor to teach me how to build conservative investment opportunities that also generate great returns.

Creating a Unique Business Strategy and Brand

Now to discuss Mach 5, my company, let me first tell you a bit about Captain Jim Murphy. Captain Murphy is an F-15 pilot who travels the world training Fortune 500 companies how to compete in today's business world. He is a supremely confident fighter pilot with world class presentation skills.

After reading his book, Flawless Execution, I decided to build my business around this "results oriented" model. What better business strategy could be used to assist clients who currently losing out on making millions simply due to a lack of action? The Flawless Execution model is all about getting it done.

Here are some Flawless Execution values in Mach 5 Real Estate:

Start with a clear future vision.
Be decisive.
Know your risks upfront and mitigate them.
Expect challenges and handle them.

Finding a World Class Real Estate Mentor

My other key mentor, David Lindahl, came into my life in 2010. Mr. Lindahl is the nation's expert for multifamily acquisition. As of this books print date, he owns over 8,250 units in multifamily. Most importantly, he was able to boldly succeed even during the 2007 meltdown by strategically focusing on the one state that would emerge – Texas. He is the author of Emerging Real Estate Markets, and his ability to select winning markets is fully proven.

Here are the Lindahl Values in Mach 5 Real Estate:
Be a very conservative investor.
Employ a low tolerance for risk.
Focus exclusively on emerging markets.
Hire the absolute best property management.

The point of me explaining my two major influences is this. Once you have established your brand and your core principals, it is easier to see if your next potential partner will meld into your vision or not. Too often you see two people with fuzzy goals thinking they have developed a direction when nothing farther from the truth could be happening.

My advice is to spend your time upfront defining your own brand and core principals. Then it will be easy to evaluate partners as an asset or hindrance to your vision.

Mach 5 Real Estate is a meld of the Flawless Execution Model I learned from Captain Jim Murphy and my multifamily business mentor David Lindahl. This combination has created a very unique brand that stands out in the marketplace. Our vision is to go beyond just meeting the financial goals of our customers and allow them to be a part of our unique vision.

Now that you have seen how to construct your own vision, we will move on to Key #3: Defining your IDEAL partner.

"Always begin with the end in mind. Knowing the outcome gives you the power to define precisely the right people to lead you there."

Joe Milunas, PMP, MSOM
Author & Multifamily Entrepreneur

Key #3: Defining your IDEAL business partner.

Picture the success of Match.com. At the core, the website uses a huge list of questions so people can actively seek out romantic partners who have values they reflect. This service is successful because it requires all the patrons to clarify what they both want and need upfront. Think how many unsuccessful marriages there are in the US today, a recent study stated 41% of first marriages fail (Forbes Magazine). The success rate of Match.com marriages is significantly higher. It is a fact that if you define what you want up front, you will have better results.

Now let us apply this to your own business. Consider you are doing proximity based partnering. I have seen it all, I have even seen people partner with someone they liked sitting next to at a boot camp. I have also seen two people join forces just to split training costs. In exchange for getting your training for less, you now have a partner you know little about. How will that person perform under pressure?

You must make it a priority to think bigger. The question to ask is not who would make a good partner, but who would make an IDEAL one. There is a critical difference. Consider there is a huge gap between good and ideal. Think of all the people you would like to model in real estate. Are any of them just good? No, these types tend to be outstanding in personality, skill, and resources. Given that, make sure you set the bar high when doing the following process.

123

**Want a Free Webinar to do this whole process step by step?
"Picking Partners" Webinar Replay:
http://Partner.mach5re.com**

As part of my tenure in my challenging master's degree, I had a project to define my ideal business partner. Below is the list I came up with, literally a full year before meeting David Harrison.

STEP 1: DEFINE

Here are list of Attributes, Resources, and Skills I made (before searching) for my ideal multifamily business partner:

1. Attributes
    a. Highly Experienced in Real Estate
    b. Conservative (w Financial Projections)
    c. Persistent

    d. Completely Honest
    e. Flexible and Coachable
    f. Charismatic
    g. Detail Oriented

2. Resources
    a. Property Resume/Ownership
    b. Excellent Credit (720+)
    c. Existing Book of Business/Clients
    d. Access to Many Off Market Deals

3. Skills
    a. Excellent Follow-through (Integrity)
    b. Excellent at Property Analysis
    c. Good Public Speaker
    d. Background in Large Transactions
    e. Knowledge in Controlling Expenses
    f. Knowledge of Property Operations
    g. World Class Problem Solving Ability

WARNING: Do not, I repeat do not settle on your list of partner attributes in particular. Your success depends on your ability to maintain this relationship no matter what circumstances appear. You will likely spend as much time with this person as your wife and children!

STEP 2: SEARCHING FOR THIS IDEAL PARTNER

You can make the most detailed and specific list of what partner would ensure your success, BUT that person must be found. This takes an active search and patience. The best way to find a partner is to look inside some high quality networking events and in your existing network. The more the events cost, the higher the caliber of the attendee.

Top 5 Places to Find Multifamily Business Partners

1. Multifamily Training Courses
2. Business Degree Programs (Particularly MBA)
3. Referrals
4. Chamber of Commerce
5. Real Estate Investment Associations

STEP 3: PARTNER DUE DILIGENCE

It is imperative, in any business where you are the financial steward of your investors' money, to have a partner you can trust. There is absolutely no replacement for a complete criminal background check. It may seem over the top, but I do this on anyone I joint venture with in real estate. Besides this obvious step, there are other critical steps you want to take to increase your odds you are joining up with the person you perceive them to be.

---

5 Partner Due Diligence Steps

1. **Background:** Do a criminal background check on Taleo.com.
2. **Competency:** Call at least four business references.
3. **Compatibility:** Spend time at a conference together.
4. **Commonality:** Discuss your goals looking for commonality.
5. **Verify Skills:** Analyze a series of properties/deals to verify competency.

MACH 5.
REAL ESTATE

> **"Trust in Allah, but tie your camel."**
>
> Arab Proverb

STEP 4: DEFINE YOUR PARTNERSHIP

Here I will show you how to specify exactly what your partnership will be doing. Going into business "together" does not cut it as a definition! Besides meeting with an attorney to draw up your agreements together (which is a must), use the list below as a framework.

Overview:

I. **The Expectations**: What will each partner provide?
II. **The Decisions**: How will large decisions be made?
III. **The Upside**: What percentage of income does each partner earn?
IV. **The Downside**: How are risk and expenses to be shared?
V. **The Scope**: Does this include all real estate or just one faucet?
VI. **The Buyout**: What if one partner chooses not to continue working?
VII. **The Breakup**: How will the existing properties and liabilities be handled?

Let's look at these in depth:

I. **The Expectations**: What will each partner provide?

This is an important part of a partnership. The key is looking at what each partner will be providing and writing it in clear language.

In our partnership in Mach 5, I am responsible for the development of our investor relationships, large group presentations, live events, webinars, and structuring our offers.

David is primarily responsible for acquisitions, which includes tapping into his huge network of clients he has (131,000+ units in his own expense reduction program). In addition, his expertise in reducing expenses is a perfect complement to my proven ability to raise revenues.

We mutually decided that his massive experience in brokerage (125 Million in closed deals) would be best utilized finding great opportunities.

One thing about expectations, it is imperative that all of the key partners participate in due diligence. To be a conservative investor, you must have direct knowledge of the investment your team is buying.

II. **The Decisions**: How will large decisions be made? It is imperative that you organize how decisions are made. I recommend putting in writing that both partners (assuming 2) need to affirmatively state they want to move forward with a transaction.

This is paramount because the partners must be in agreement as they are both responsible for the outcome and providing the results to the investors.

III. **The Upside**: What percentage of income does each management partner earn of the company?
In our company, we decided on a straight 50% split of upside with each of us providing 50% of the capital. I believe in being fair, yet setting high expectations for each other.

IV. **The Downside**: How are risk and expenses to be shared? There are sunk costs in deals that end up not working out. It is important to define exactly how these will be shared in the management team. Examples include legal expenses, trips to the property, inspections, etc.

V. **The Scope**: Does this include all real estate or just one faucet? Say you form a company to buy real estate with a partner. Things go well and a few years in you buy an apartment building using all of your own funds. Is this in the scope of your partnership? Can the partners invest independently of the main company you have together? This is a key discussion to have.

VI. **The Buyout**: What if one partner chooses not to continue working?
What if one of the partners decides to not want to continue in real estate? This is hard to define because there are different levels of effort. The key is to define what would trigger a partner's ability to do a buyout and to hopefully avoid that.

VII. **The Breakup**: How will the existing properties and liabilities be handled?

All partnerships must define their dissolution, whether it happen in a year or even 30 years down the road. It generally makes sense to define that all properties will continue.

"Treat employees like they make a difference and they will."

Jim Goodnight – CEO of SAS

KEY #4: Hire the best team members your project can justify.

After you have organized your leadership team the next step is to develop a great team to accomplish your goals. In order to operate this team effectively, you must first start by choosing the right vendors and people to join your team.

Robert Kiyosaki, author of Rich Dad Poor Dad, is a great mentor on having the right mindset for hiring team members. In his book he explains that good entrepreneurs tend to hire top performing advisors. At Mach 5, we have adopted this same mindset. We currently have world class advisors and have been trained in the most expensive, yet highest value training in the real estate industry.

Robert Kiyosaki takes this concept further by stating, "an intelligent person hires people who are more intelligent than he is." This implies that the leader must demonstrate the confidence to admit there are areas where he/she must not be afraid to hire advisors who have a higher level of mastery. This is in contrast to a leader who is intimidated by the competency of others.

We employ Kiyosaki's concepts in our own company and suggest you do the same. If you carefully budget for better staffing, the results will show. Studies done by the Institute of Real Estate Management show that, "buildings run by certified managers have higher occupancy." The better rent collections and occupancy more than pay for hiring good people to assist. In essence, good people pay for themselves.

Here are three examples of why you should hire better people:

Property Managers

- Results will vary widely in this area. The key to getting a great property manager is to visit the properties they have under management. Make sure they manage the same building type as you will be buying. We prefer to use highly talented property managers with experience handling construction projects. The IREM.org website is a fantastic resource to start.

- Please note: If you go cheap on the property management, beware. This is the core member of your team to ensure the investment is successful.

- Make sure to also hire property managers who agree to be paid based on collected rents. Typically only the competent candidates will agree to this clause.

Contractors

- There are some key reasons to be very careful about selecting contractors. When a competitive bid situation is happening, contractors will often discount their bids. This can be good, except that often the most desperate contractor often bids the lowest. Then these cash starved contractors can run out of cash to pay their sub-contractors... not good for your project at all. I recommend using referrals to work only with the contractors who are stable, reliable, and cost efficient.

Attorneys

- There are securities laws that must be adhered to when raising funds to buy properties. Non specialized attorneys take longer to get your documents done. This can cost you the deal. I prefer working with a licensed syndication attorney named Gene Trowbridge who I have known over five years. Mr. Trowbridge's team makes the process for our investors to join our deals simple, transparent, and timely.

- As an added level of service, great attorneys will give the investor the convenience of being able to sign the documents online and save time. When a good deal is opened, savvy investors want the ability to quickly review and submit documents online before losing their spot to someone else.

Checklist to hire OUTSTANDING vendors

- ✓ Define their purpose/role.
- ✓ Determine your budget.
- ✓ Contact your network for referrals.
- ✓ Setup appointments a minimum of 3 vendors.
- ✓ Get references and call them. ***MVP***
- ✓ Criminal Background Check. (Taleo.com – 9.95)
- ✓ Select the best candidate.

KEY #5: Document your team's successes and tell the world!

We live in a "prove it to me" world now. According to the University of Texas A & M, "a conservative estimate has the average American consumer exposed to more than 850 commercial messages a day." Due to this saturation, people have become skeptical. For any company to do well in these circumstances, it is imperative to make it easy for your new prospective clients to verify company successes.

Our company has a list of successes ranging from awesome deals we have completed to David's clients he has saved hundreds of thousands of dollars though expense reduction. The key though is ensuring that our investor clients can access proof of these successes.

I must say that until I actually got the letter from David's previous boss, did I truly 100% believe he had closed $125,000,000 in real estate deals. Once he provided that, I realized that everything he told me was true. Yes, it is like striking gold. Not only is it great to have someone like David as a partner, but having the proof to actually show investors is just as valuable.

Everyone is looking for proof of competency. Given this fact, we have spent time documenting our company's successes. Our website is www.mach5re.com There you will find a complete booklet of testimonial letters as well as how our business works. Whether you choose us or someone else, you can use our information as a benchmark of what investors, just like you, are looking for when picking a multifamily team to grow their money.

I wanted to take a second and acknowledge your commitment to being a better person and investor. Spending the time to learn how to choose great partners is absolutely key to getting to your own real estate goals faster and easier than going out alone.

The next step for you is to watch the webinar above. You will learn the step by step mechanics of picking a good partner. Also, you will get to know our own criteria for our investor partners as a bonus. Our large deals require investor partners who are interested in earning good cash flow and potential appreciation on their invested money. Watching this webinar is as important as breathing oxygen, your financial future depends on it!

Lastly, email me at Joe@mach5re.com if you would like to get direct access to our "done for you" multifamily investments, #1 ranked expense reduction services, or just for advice on choosing partners.

Toast to great partnerships!

Joe Milunas, PMP, MSOM
Owner, Mach 5 Real Estate
www.Mach5re.com

Joe Milunas, PMP, MSOM
Owner, Mach 5 Real Estate
Passive Multifamily Investments
Testimonials: www.mach5re.com
Email: joe@mach5re.com
Office: 949-872-9434

What investors like you are saying:

"Based on evidence of his consistent performance, I would recommend utilizing Joe Milunas and MACH 5 for your real estate investment goals."
Sheri Sears – Acquisitions Dir. - Invest Club for Women

"David Harrison was able to save us $480,000 in reduced expenses by auditing our 18,000 unit multifamily portfolio."
John Gilmore, Hamilton-Zanze Investments

"Lastly and most importantly, this relationship is profitable and produces results."
Tom Linovitz, Owner of Pacific Mortgage Group

Your *Hidden Millions* for Real Estate Deals

Lane McGhee

How to find or create money to acquire real estate properties.

In this chapter I'll share twenty-one creative financing strategies, tried and true, proven methods being used right now in the multi-family residential market that allow you to Find, Finesse, and Fund your real estate deals with Little or No Money from your own pocket.

I'll also summarize the latest exciting developments and new rules approved for Crowd Funding, an up and coming new marketing channel to access capital online from anyone around the world.

By Lane McGhee, Economist & Real Estate Entrepreneur
www.YourHiddenMillions.com

Where can you come up with "millions" of dollars to get real estate deals done? There are many creative ways, and several "hidden" strategies you can use to uncover or reveal the funds needed to close real estate deals. Nearly everyone has heard the "No Money Down" hype so easily talked about, yet seemingly difficult to accomplish. Don't get me wrong, there are real "no money down" deals done, even today, and the purpose of this chapter is to explore workable methods to create or find the "hidden millions" you can use to fund your real estate deals, large or small, or anywhere in between.

Here's my definition of creative financing: (a) a method of creating funds to expedite acquiring an asset; (b) alternative ways to enable funding and purchasing real property.

Recently, a broker friend of mine contacted me about a multi-family property for sale. I had no available capital – zero – but it was a good deal, so I took a look. After analyzing the numbers, we wrote an offer, accepted their counter, and scheduled the inspection.

All the while thinking, "How the heck am I going to pay for this?" The property needed some repairs, so we proposed that the owner carry back a loan for 3 years to allow us the time and cash flow needed for repairs. We ultimately agreed on 20% down, owner financing for 18 months, and a 5% price reduction to help offset the repair cost. I had to borrow from family for that 20% down, and was able to acquire the property.

On the day we closed just ten days later, we had over $75,000 in new equity and were set to make a net $600 per month *after* all expenses and debt service… not bad for a quick deal completed in less than 3 weeks with zero dollars out-of-pocket!

Think about that for a moment. If you did a deal like that every month, you'd be a millionaire in just over a year! And you'd be making over $80,000 per year in extra income. (Heck, even if you did just one deal like that each year, and you'd be a millionaire in only 10 years.) And you will have achieved all that because you took positive action, even though you had no money in your pocket.

I'm doing it… so can you! Is there more to it? Sure, there is more to learn and more to do. And if you're willing to learn and take action, you can do it.

If you want to create real economic wealth in real estate, even with none of your own money, even without stellar credit, read on.

The American Economy is the greatest in the world: individuals and businesses pursue their self-interests, which blossom and benefit the general well-being of all. Even when the economy is depressing or recessing, marvelous opportunities seem to magically appear for those who are willing to look, learn, and leap into action. It's not really magic: it takes vision, verve and vigor to get up and walk while others are sitting around, or to run when others are still walking. First it takes will. Do you have the will to become actively wealthy in real estate? Want to discover where your real estate wealth is hiding?

While it may not happen overnight, with sustained willingness to do what it takes to keep on moving forward, humans can achieve what their minds can conceive! What can you conceive? Napoleon Hill wrote his famous book, "Think and Grow Rich," on the premise that people like you and me can use our brains and open our minds to ways we can grow and prosper. What real estate success can you think up for yourself? When we actualize our thoughts into goals and achievements, we can profitably pursue and accomplish great things.

So what's holding you back?

Do you remember as a school kid what you looked forward to when you were in class? Recess, of course; break time. Right? So why, as adults, are we so willing to badmouth an Economic Recess? Just because journalists, politicians, and pundits call it a Recession, and say it's bad news, does that define a truth for you personally? They just want something to blame for bad news, so they label as "bad" an absolutely normal economic cyclical downturn, and tell you to whine and not spend money, which makes things even worse, and on it goes.

Have you ever noticed that it's not the *National* Economy, but your *Personal* Economy that matters most? And when prices go down, as they often do in a recession, isn't that technically a good time to "buy low" so you can "sell high" later? Sure, but what if you lose your job? Well that means it's high time to backstop that job loss with cash flow from real estate! Find an economically emerging market, and buy real estate.

But how can you buy real estate when you have no money? Or perhaps poor credit?

Whether the economy is strengthening, weakening, or just stagnating as it so often does, traditional real estate lending tightens and loosens in market cycles right along with the economy, usually in opposition to what's needed in the market.

Have you ever noticed that banks and lenders tighten up just when real estate entrepreneurs really need funding for deals? And traditional lending finally loosens up only after deal-funding has become relatively easy to get in the alternative funding arena?

Thank goodness for hard money lenders, private lenders, partnerships, syndications, joint ventures, and loan brokers who have developed their own direct funding sources in addition to banks! But even with these sources, you typically need at least some "skin in the game" in the form of your own cash or capital. However, here's more good news: there are many alternative funding sources where you need little or none of your own money to close a deal.

Want to explore today's alternative funding sources? A number of non-traditional, non-bank, creative financing sources have blossomed, and online Crowd Funding is starting to sizzle. It's all about economic leverage, at a very personal level. And you can do it; where there's a will, there's a way.

Let's examine the 21 Top Creative Finance methods being used by real estate entrepreneurs and investors right now in today's market. I use these strategies for my real estate deals, as do many of my real estate buddies. To me it all boils down to variations on three basic leverage categories that I call (A) "Seller Leverage," (B) "Connection Leverage," and (C) "Extra Leverage."

Category A: Seller Leverage – where Buyer directly leverages Seller to finance the deal.

This is my favorite category, and often the first and easiest to implement. It involves leveraging the Seller or in other words, closing the deal by having the current Owner facilitate the funding. I'll share eight variations or strategies that Leverage the Seller in the transaction to close a deal. As you study these strategies, #1-#8 below, realize that most often, there is no Buyer qualifying, no credit checking required in a Seller Leverage transaction.

1. **Seller Financing** – also called Owner Financing or Carry Back Loan, Mortgage or Note.

   How do you know if a Seller is willing to carry a note to finance the transaction? You present a proposal and ask! Or better yet, you make sure your broker is educated on how to strategically ask a Seller about carrying a note. Many Sellers will not be interested, but it doesn't hurt to ask; often a Seller doesn't understand what exactly is involved or is uncertain how to proceed. Once they understand the benefits to them, a Seller is more apt to accept a deal where they initially participate to make it happen.

   The Seller Carry works best where the seller is motivated to sell a property quickly, or where the property exhibits significant deferred maintenance issues, when it's in disrepair and may be difficult to qualify for bank financing, or where it's simply a burden to the current owner. Perhaps it represents an undesired annoyance to an absentee or out-of-state owner.

The Seller Carry Back can only happen when a Seller is willing and able to carry back a loan based on price and terms mutually agreeable; it must be negotiated as a win-win, not as a "trick" or attempt to take unfair advantage in either direction. Seller Carries are used for (a) quick closings, (b) typically at higher-than-market interest rate, or (c) higher-than-market price, or (d) when a buyer cannot get conventional financing, or (e) whenever a special leverage opportunity can be structured into a property purchase.

2. **Master Lease with Purchase Option** – two separate contracts: a Lease, and an Option.

In an event where a Seller is highly motivated, but a Buyer doesn't have funds or enough credit, a Seller and Buyer may profitably consider a Master Lease Purchase Option (two contracts).

A master lease contract allows Buyer to lease the entire property and take over operations (e.g., rent collection and management) by paying mutually agreed payments over a mutually agreed term. The payment(s) will, at minimum, cover the cost of any current mortgage, taxes, and insurance so that there is no out-of-pocket cost to the current owner. Plus there is typically a percentage share of net positive cash flow negotiated, which would allow positive cash flow to be shared in some proportion with both parties during the term of agreement.

An Option is a Buyer's "right" to purchase an item at a set price, coupled with a Seller's "obligation" to sell that item in the future at that set price, in exchange for payment of a non-refundable fee today. A purchase option contract, then, is a second contract that, for a fee, locks in a fixed price for the property to be purchased in the future within a certain term, typically 3-5 years. The option must be exercised by the Buyer (financed and closed) within that term or the option expires, the Buyer's right forfeited, and the Seller's obligation ended with title retained by the original owner.

This Master Lease - Purchase Option strategy is used for (a) quick closings, (b) often at higher-than-market interest rate, or (c) higher-than-market price, or (d) when a buyer cannot get conventional financing, or (e) whenever a special leverage opportunity can be structured into a transaction, and (f) when both parties can benefit from the arrangement.

3. **Property Equity Transaction** – sometimes called a Leveraged Buyout.

When a Seller is highly motivated, a Buyer can sometimes acquire the property using a short-term Seller Carry Note, sometimes with additional outside short-term loans, typically for a short period of 3-12 months, with the intent to refinance as quickly as possible. "Seasoning" comes into play here – there must either be enough value added, or enough time elapsed, to warrant a higher appraised value of the property (or equity) at the time of refinancing.

Then, the Buyer remedies cosmetic distress, resolves property management problems, or makes needed repairs. After repairs, Buyer refinances the property to take cash out at an amount sufficient to (a) repay Seller Note, and (b) repay other short-term financing or repair costs.

This strategy can be used to flip a property after renovation, or to gain paper equity quickly to refinance and hold the property. This strategy is most effective in an up-trending market, but can be disastrous if done in an unexpected down-turn after acquisition, as refinancing is dependent on a higher property value several months in the future, after the initial transaction.

4. **Wrap loan** – where Seller carries a new loan that "wraps" around the original loan.

When a Seller has a lower-interest loan, and Buyer is willing to pay a higher-interest rate, this strategy creates positive cash flow for Seller. Seller can offer Buyer a new loan, while keeping and paying down the original mortgage loan; i.e., the new loan "wraps" around the owner's original loan.

The new Wrap loan would typically be made at a higher interest rate, with a higher loan amount, so that the original owner can enjoy positive cash flow, higher equity, and command a higher market price and higher down payment by offering this type of Seller Financing.

The Buyer benefits by being able to close quickly, pay a fair interest rate, and a fair market price on the property, acquiring it more easily than going through traditional financing.

This strategy may also be used for a property difficult to sell, or in a distressed case of being "under water" in the current loan(s). In this case, Seller may let the property go for the current outstanding loan balance, or at only a slight premium, or possibly even at a discount.

Buyer Risk: the discount strategy is often used when the property condition is so poor that it cannot qualify for traditional financing.

However, if a Buyer is able to renovate and rehabilitate a property to make it profitable, a Seller without the means or desire to renovate can discount the purchase price and Wrap the loan to be rid of the property.

5. **Loan Assumption** – where the current mortgage loan(s) may be assumed by a new Buyer.

Where a Buyer has quality credit, but little cash, the Loan Assumption strategy can often play a critical role in acquiring a profitable property.

The Loan Assumption typically requires credit qualification on the Buyer. Loan Assumption is used where the Seller is motivated and has assumable financing in place. Arrangements are made with bank, and Buyer assumes making the Seller's payments, often with little or no down payment.

Not all loans are assumable, and not all Buyers can qualify to assume loans. Buyer risk: sellers are sometimes motivated to sell due to substandard property condition and may know about, but not disclose, cracked foundations, or other unseen deficiencies. Due diligence and thorough inspection is always recommended.

6. **Subject-to** – similar to Loan Assumption, but not qualified by or sanctioned by the bank.

Buyer may find an Owner highly motivated to sell due to financial hardship, family illness or death, substandard property condition or other distress. Seller may simply offer to walk away and allow a Buyer to take over making the current mortgage loan payments, with little or no down payment, convey the property deed and transfer title to Buyer.

The purchase contract in this case is an arrangement "subject to" Buyer making all loan payments in full faith and confidence. It typically requires no qualifying of the Buyer, nor notification to the bank. With the "subject to" contract arrangement, title is transferred to Buyer, often via a trust arrangement, and is contingent upon the new owner making all bank loan payments on time for the rest of the loan term, or, until that loan is refinanced by Buyer, or the property sold to pay off the original loan.

However, in the interim, there is also a risk of triggering the "due on sale" clause in the underlying loan contract.

The Risk of "due on sale" arises when the loan contract contains a clause stating that "upon sale or transfer of title, the loan becomes due and payable in full" immediately. If Buyer, the new title holder, has no funds to pay off that loan, the property could be foreclosed and all could be lost, including a foreclosure added to the Buyer's credit report.

Further, if the foreclosed property is sold and the sale price doesn't cover the full balance of the loan, a deficiency judgment can be filed against the new and unsuspecting Buyer, personally, for the difference now owed, which could be tens of thousands of dollars, or in some cases much more.

Nevertheless, banks are not anxious to foreclose on undervalued properties, and as long as regular payments are consistently made on time, it is unlikely that banks will research title transfers without cause. But a Buyer needs to go into a "subject to" deal with eyes wide open, understand the risks, and have a solid exit strategy or specific time frame to refinance and pay off the original underlying loan. "Subject To" arrangements can carry substantial risk to both parties, and should only be entered when all risks are fully understood. (Consult attorney.)

7. **Contract for Deed** – where title is retained by Seller, until Buyer pays off Seller Note.

The contract-for-deed strategy is used when an underqualified or inexperienced Buyer finds a Seller willing to carry a note, but unwilling to take the risk of transferring title to such an underqualified Buyer, until that Buyer proves worthy by repaying the Seller's loan.

The Buyer agrees to a type of Seller financing where a Seller carry-back promissory note is signed, and a purchase contract is also signed, but the Seller retains the property deed and title does not transfer to Buyer until that Seller carry mortgage contract is repaid in full.

When the Seller Financing Contract is fully repaid (or refinanced), that loan contract payoff is traded for the property deed and full transfer of title to Buyer.

Contract-for-deed is typically used when a Buyer has little or no collateral, credit history, or experience, but exhibits an absolute willingness to repay the loan. Buyer Risk: in the event of a late payment or other default, Buyer can be forced to vacate the property if the default cannot be cured within the timeframe specified in the contract, and thereby cause Buyer to lose all monies paid toward that property.

Basically, in the case of buyer default, all payments made are deemed as rent, and are not returned, Buyer vacates the property, and original owner retains title and any improvements made to the property. (Consult attorney.)

8. **Seller Second** – where Buyer obtains primary loan, but still needs funds to close.

A Buyer may be able to obtain a Seller Second Mortgage loan after a Buyer gets primary funding (perhaps a loan from friends or relatives, or via traditional first mortgage) that covers a large portion of the purchase price, but not enough to cover the full price of the property.

After a Buyer and Seller have finalized a purchase contract, the Buyer's financing comes up short and Buyer proposes that the Seller step in to make up the difference using a Second Mortgage Note. For example, a Buyer may have enough cash and financing to secure 75% to 90% of the funds needed, but he still needs 10% to 25% to close the deal.

If the Seller is highly motivated, or has enough confidence in the Buyer, the Seller agrees to carry the funds needed to close in exchange for a promissory note in the amount of that remaining balance. Since this note is in second position (higher risk) to the primary or senior note, the interest rate will likely be substantially higher, and the term will likely be shorter.
Bonus: Short Sale – where a Seller offers to sell a property "short" of the balance owed.

Granted, this may not sound like a Seller Finance strategy, as most often a Short Sale purchase price must be approved by the bank or entity holding the mortgage note on the property. However, there are many strategies that can be implemented with a current Owner/Seller to preclude a foreclosure, forestall a short sale, or even to *facilitate* a short sale, all prior to the Bank dictating the terms of a sale. And a discount price certainly represents leverage in a deal.

Therefore, we have added the Short Sale as an opportunity alert: when a Seller may be in a financial hardship situation, an astute Buyer may be able to find a way to turn a particular Seller's lemon into lemonade, by negotiating directly with that Seller.

One idea is offering to buy the underlying mortgage note from the current lien-holder. If the note-holder is a bank or institution, note purchase may be difficult (or impossible), but there are times when the note-holder is open to selling that note, at a discount, to a qualified buyer.

More traditionally, both the Seller and Lien-holder (bank) must agree to a Short Sale price, as the lien-holder must accept that price as payment in full, even though that price is 'short' of the outstanding balance. Short Sales are often made to avoid the time and cost of a full foreclosure.

On the other hand, purchasing a Short Sale allows the Buyer to pay a discounted price for the property, and could create immediate equity or significant profit after repairs are made. Thereby, substantial leverage is often built into the deal. Occasionally you can find a multi-family property Short Sale, so don't be shy: dive in and try to negotiate your great deal!

Case Study 1

That wraps up our discussion on Seller Leverage strategies, although there are many more variations you can negotiate. Having covered the first 8 strategies, we have 13 more to study. But first, may I share with you a deal recently closed, using a few of my favorite strategies?

In our local Real Estate Investment club meeting in San Diego, I met a wonderful woman named Diane. We met after I made an announcement at the San Diego club about opportunities to partner with me on multi-family deals in Phoenix. She sought me out to follow up on my announcement.

We got to talking and learned that Diane owned a 6-unit multi-family property in Phoenix near one of my properties. We agreed to stay in touch and talk again later. At the next REI club meeting, we found each other again, exchanged greetings, and I asked how things were going with her Phoenix property. She frowned, looked down at the floor and said, "You know, I wish I knew. Being here in San Diego and not owning other properties in Phoenix, I'm just not doing anything with that property." Her body language said it all… the Phoenix property was a headache and an annoyance for her.

I asked if she was interested in off-loading the property. She perked up and asked what I had in mind. I told her I'd like to take a look at the property, review the financials, and I just might be interested in owning it. She responded affirmatively and I followed up with a written proposal the next day. Having developed a budding friendship with Diane, I knew she really wanted to get rid of that property. However she was a savvy real estate broker and didn't want to let go at too low a price.

My proposal offered the current market price range and called for a seller carryback loan with reasonable down payment, higher than market interest rate, and a term of 48 months.

A few days later she called and said she liked my proposal, but that the price range was too low. I provided her with a full comparative market analysis from my Phoenix broker as well as Phoenix Metro statistics from LoopNet and other online sources. See decided to give her two broker friends in Phoenix a call and get a BPO (Broker's Price Opinion) on her property. I said, "Great, let's touch base after you've got that information."

A couple weeks later she received the BPO stating a price range of $300k-$325k. In my opinion those BPOs were way too high for the then-current market, but those pie-in-the-sky numbers obviously sounded good to a Seller.

While she conceded that the BPOs were not supported with any comps or hard data, she really liked those numbers. She wanted something close to $325k while market comps were suggesting a price somewhere around $270k. Obviously we had quite a wide range to cover.

On my next trip to Phoenix I received permission to inspect the property. We met her property manager at the site and entered several of the units. The property includes two triplexes set on one lot. It turns out that both roofs had been poorly patched after being severely damaged in a hail storm, and the overall roofing was old, thin, and sorely in need of replacement. We also found an insect infestation, substantial deferred maintenance issues needing immediate attention, along with windows, fixtures and appliances requiring repair or replacement.

Contractors came back with repair cost estimates totaling $36,000 with the roof replacement accounting for half of that number. Re-roofing and making the interior repairs would definitely add value to the property, allowing us to raise rents and increase cash flow.

So I took that cost estimate number and offered a restructured price proposal starting at $325k, subtracting out the 6% Real Estate Commission since this was going to be a "for sale by owner" transaction. Removing the commission took the number down to $305,500 and further subtracting the $36,000 cost estimate brought the adjusted price to $269,500 once again justifying my price point at $270,000.

We met at a local Denny's to go over my proposal. Diane appreciated the proposal, and was willing to make some adjustment for repair issues, but stated she just couldn't go below $280k, even considering the repairs needed.

We emailed, and telephoned, teased and cajoled over the next couple days. Finally, we agreed to *her* price with *my* terms: $280k with 10% down, split the closing costs, define the purchase "as is, where is, with all faults," and she'd carry a loan for 48 months so we could close quickly.

In other words, I take all the property risks and remove the property headaches from her forever, while she carries a favorable loan at her deemed price – win-win. Mutually agreed, it was time to open escrow.

Now I had to come up with the 10% down payment of $28,000. I needed cash reserves to pay for repairs, so how in the world was I going to come up with that much cash?

I applied for 6 new credit cards, and got 4. These cards allowed 'balance transfer' checks at 0% APR for 12 months, and charged 3% balance transfer fees. I viewed the balance transfer fees like "points" in a mortgage or lending situation, and was more than happy to pay those points to secure this property with a down payment at 0% interest.

Then, I could use the rental income cash flow to start the needed repairs, as well as find a roofing company that would finance the roof (or put that expense on a 12-month 0% APR credit card).

We completed the purchase agreement paperwork, opened escrow with $28,000 in credit card checks for the down payment, and closed the deal a couple weeks later.

I suppose you could call this a "no money down" deal with a credit card twist. No matter how you look at it, I got this property financed 100%, using other people's money, with no cash out of my pocket.

Did you know you could use Credit Cards to buy real estate?

Category B: Connection Leverage – where Buyer leverages Connections to finance a deal.

Buyers who learn to leverage personal influence among their connections can become dynamos and very successful. Once you succeed at something, you want to tell other people, and then have them tell the world, and you start by sharing with your own connections: business associates, social circles, social media, friends, relatives and family members.

We can leverage our connections through personal influence, or credit, or both, to enhance our ability to acquire real estate. Connection Leverage is often lumped in with using Other People's Money, "OPM" (sometimes likened to "opium" – pain release, very addictive – but we won't get into that).

While these connection leverage strategies utilize other peoples or third-party monetary means, these techniques also can directly obligate the Buyer's credit and character.

The funding sources named below may be full-recourse, non-recourse, or a combination of both, based on certain criteria, as specified in a contract.

"Recourse" refers to personal liability and the ability of a third party to collect a debt against the personal means, income, or assets of an individual, partner, spouse, or family, to the extent that the value of repossession or foreclosure doesn't cover the debt.

"Non-recourse" protects individuals from personal liability and any ability of a third party to collect on a debt from personal means, income or assets, other than the property asset or collateral that secured the original debt being repossessed or foreclosed. Non-recourse debt is therefore highly desirable, although not always available.

Let's look at the following eight Connection Leverage strategies, #9 - #16, and see which ones you can use.

9. **Credit Cards** – Buyer can use credit card or "paper checks" to get cash easily and quickly.

Credit Cards are making a comeback after the Great Recession, and competing to get your business. Many credit cards allow for balance transfers or 'checks' to be written; especially brand new cards, which carry a low promotional interest rate, usually 0.0%, with low or no fees for some period of time, often 12-18 months.

A credit card 'check' allows the user to turn credit into cash that can be used toward a down payment or repairs or both.

During the Great Recession, credit was tightened, and many people's credit limits were drastically cut, but that era is now over. Don't get me wrong, credit card use requires credit honesty, and of course, credit extended needs to be eventually paid back. But isn't it nice to know there's a pocket resource where you can get temporary cash needed to get a real estate deal done?

With financial reform laws enacted and implemented, credit card companies have developed special programs now available whereby one can strategically obtain multiple credit card lines with promotional rates for both personal, and business, and corporate credit card accounts. And many of these available business cards are non-recourse, offering low or no interest rates for approximately a year, with low or no fees.

Even when there are fees assessed, typical charges for a balance transfer are about 3%, similar to loan origination points for private lenders, and lower than most hard money loans.

Certain credit card programs can be predatory, while others are extremely friendly. Because these programs change over time, we can't list the best cards here, but if you'd like to know the credit cards we use and recommend, feel free to contact me, or visit our website.

Personal credit cards are typically full recourse, while business and corporate cards can be structured to have recourse to the business only, while non-recourse to the individual person or owner of the business.

Credit cards cannot be over-extended without negative consequences, so each time credit is used for any purpose, the situation must be analyzed and a solid repayment plan formulated in order to avoid nightmares, on the way to achieving your real estate dreams.

In my opinion, this type of credit should only be used to improve appreciating assets that actively generate income, and never for consumable products or depreciating consumer items such as vehicles, clothes, vacations, or toys.

10. Relatives and Friends – whether last resort, or prime target: Relatives are resources.

When real estate entrepreneurs tap relatives or friends, we typically feel a personal obligation to ensure they are repaid, and are properly treated. Therefore, I categorize family and friends under Connection Leverage, because if there ever is a loss, one way or another, you are going to feel the obligation, and you are going to want to have their backs.

Rather than asking for money, a savvy Real Estate Entrepreneur will approach relatives and friends to let them know what he's doing, and how he's having fun these days.

This is where leveraging personal influence is more important than wielding credit. And this is decidedly not braggadocio... it's just fun! Buying real estate, enjoying passive income for yourself, and earning solid returns for investors makes for great conversation in certain places, at certain times.

Social media is a great place to let people know what you are up to, in addition to conversations at personal gatherings or social meet-ups.

When they ask what you're up to, and hear you talk about what you're doing, some few relatives or friends may want to participate as investors, but most will also be able to refer you to others who might be interested in high returns, a second income, passive income, or real estate investments. The question to ask: "Do you know anyone interested in making solid returns, or extra income, secured by real estate investing?" Then be ready to take down names and numbers.

11.Investors or Sponsors – where a Buyer can leverage profitable deals to raise capital.

Every Buyer must have something of value to leverage or "trade" whenever he invites another party to invest something of value in a deal or venture. How do you structure a deal? How much does the Buyer get? How much does an Investor get? How is a Sponsor compensated?

These are questions whose answers are determined by the respective values brought to the negotiating table. For a Buyer, what do you have of value to leverage or trade? For example, if you "find" a deal that proves profitable, that could be worth a Finder fee.

If you've analyzed a deal and know the detailed location, condition, value add, profitability and cash flow scenarios that information could be worth an Underwriting fee. If you're able to put a property under contract, after finding and analyzing, that could be worth a minority Partnership percentage.

If you need a Sponsor to pay a deposit or sign the loan with you, that Sponsor will require compensation or a certain Partnership percentage. If you bring Investors to the table, via

Offering Circular or Private Placement Memorandum (paperwork done by attorney), that could be worth an Acquisition fee, or a Management Partnership percentage.

Sponsors are typically high net worth individuals, who are willing to sign loan docs with Buyer, and who can bring either capital or additional investors into a deal, in return for a Partnership percentage for both the Sponsor and the Investors. And, of course, each Investor will receive either a partnership percentage or an interest payment, depending on whether they are Equity or Debt Investors.

The deal structure and partnership percentage depend on the elements of value each party brings to the deal.

Bringing Sponsors or Investors into deals is often called Syndication or Joint Venture, and these arrangements require SEC compliance. Real Estate Entrepreneurs seek to leverage their personal influence by constantly presenting opportunities to others. For example, you can attend networking events, meet-ups, REI Clubs, or seminars to build relationships with accredited investors or others willing to invest in a venture, loan money, or sponsor a deal.

After all, you're not trying to fund the entire purchase price, but only an amount that covers the down payment and necessary pre-paid cash expenses closing costs, origination points, acquisition fees, or other closing expenses.

12.Equity and Debt Partners – contributors seeking ownership equity or interest payments

Buyers can choose to seek Equity Partners in deals to minimize interest and debt service payments and to manage cash flow to achieve specific goals. Some equity partners will participate in a deal in order to receive returns through long-term appreciation in the value of an asset over time.

Other equity partners will prefer to receive a percentage of net positive cash flow from inception. Typically, equity partners will receive distributions of both: cash flow over time, and equity appreciation at the time of disposition or sale. Buyers will bring on partners who receive an equity share as a percentage of the deal, commensurate with their level of investment. SEC compliance is required, but easy enough and straight-forward to do.

Buyers can also choose to bring on <u>Debt Partners</u> who lend money based on an interest rate, and who may, or may not, participate in ownership equity (typically at lower % than equity partners). Debt partners may desire interest-only payments followed by a "balloon" repayment of principal, or they may prefer an amortized payment stream with principal plus interest.

Deals can be structured in different ways with different repayment schedules, such as no payments for an initial period of up to a year, with regular payments commencing thereafter. Deals can be structured for either short periods of time, or over a longer term.

Typically, debt partners have a primary desire to receive fixed payments for a specified time period, and are less interested in equity or appreciation in value. Sometimes, buyers prefer debt partners where the amount of ownership equity distribution is limited or restricted, thus yielding a greater amount of equity ownership for Buyer and principal parties.

SEC compliance is required, but easy enough and straight-forward to do.

13.Private Lenders – privately available funds at reasonable rates, as negotiated privately

Private lenders are often compared to, and confused with, Hard Money lenders. Both Private Lenders and Hard Money lenders are typically "asset-based" lenders, usually non-recourse to Buyer personally, but this is not always the case. In virtually every other respect, "Private" and "Hard Money" are different.

Private lenders are, well, private. They could be family members, friends, a business colleague, or perhaps even a small business or professional lender who specializes in private or direct-sourced funds for lending, as opposed to institutional monetary lending sources like banks. Private Lenders may have lending guidelines, but the deal you strike will be negotiated privately between you and the Private Lender; terms and conditions will reflect what you two parties find mutually agreeable.

You'll need to network and develop your own private lending sources, or do some pains-taking research to locate private lenders, since they are "private" after all. You may also find private lending sources through referrals and references from other real estate entrepreneurs. Or you may develop your own private lending sources through outreach and ongoing contact with family and friends to receive loans from your own circle of friends and associates. Private Lenders are usually more flexible, with lower interest rates and have lower origination cost.

Private Loans are "asset-based," which means they are non-recourse loans, instead based on the value of a real estate asset acquired or improved with the proceeds of the loan. A lien is often placed on the property.

14. **Hard money lenders** – high-cost funds easily available for short-term loans

There's a difference between Hard Money Lenders and Private Lenders, although they are often compared to each other and frequently confused.

Hard Money lenders typically charge high origination points, usually for a limited term loan of about three months. If a loan goes beyond that limited time frame, they charge another set of points just as if you're originating a new loan when you enter the fourth month. While Hard Money interest rates are relatively high, the point cost is the most onerous.

So why do real estate entrepreneurs borrow Hard Money?

"Hard Money" almost seems like a misnomer, in that these loans represent Easy Money and are easily available. If you do an online search of Hard Money Lenders, chances are high that you'll find several Hard Money sources right in your own community. If not, there are many more online, fully accessible.

Why would real estate investors pay high points and high interest rates for these short-term loans?

Because they need funds to repair or renovate quickly, and can make far more money from profits after repositioning a property. Hard Money Loans tend to be very short-term, and have a very good record of repayment history since, in the event of default, the lender can take over the property, complete the repairs themselves, and sell the property at a profit.

For multi-family properties, Hard Money lenders are sometimes used to pay Earnest Money Deposits in order to close a deal quickly, which allows additional time to secure investors and partners to obtain full funding for the deal, and then repay the hard money loan.

Finally, Hard Money lenders typically have very specific criteria for granting loans, standardized forms, and defined ratios. They are asset-based lenders, so the primary collateral or security is the property asset or subject of the loan.

15. **Collateral from other properties** – use of other property assets to secure funding for a deal

Another way to secure credit or funds for acquiring a new deal is to allow a Lender to use equity from other properties or assets owned, allowing liens to be placed on those other-owned properties and assets. While this may not seem like a leverage strategy at first, one may be able to leverage $100,000 equity from one property, to secure a $500,000 new loan on another property.

Further, using collateral to secure a new loan may be a short-term strategy to allow acquisition of a property so it can be renovated and repositioned, then sold or flipped several months to a year later, and realize a nice profit margin along with the cash flow.

16. **Interest-only Loans** – allows smaller payments in early years, with balloon payment at term

Interest-only payments have been around for a long time.

And it's well known that one can have substantially lower monthly payments in the early years of ownership. Lower payments allow cash flow to be used for needed repairs or capital expenditures, in order to improve property, raise rents, and increase asset value, which is an important strategy.

Today, multi-family financing is becoming more competitive, with ever more options, including Interest-only payment options for 3, 5, or even 7 years. But the Buyer has to ask for the Interest-only option in order to factor it into the acquisition deal structure. In addition, the exit strategy must be evaluated, since a balloon payment will be due and payable at the end of the interest-only period, and may force a property disposition and sale.

The interest-only payment structure is used to leverage cash flow in the early years, and then refinance when equity is built up, before the balloon payment comes due.

Case Study 2

Here's a story out of Atlanta, Georgia where my friend, Bill, was looking for a 100-plus apartment building for sale. He had no money of his own, but wanted to acquire a large apartment house. This is his story…

Hi Lane,

You asked how I acquired this apartment building, and I had to get creative to do it. It's an amazing deal. I was focused on acquiring a large apartment building. In my search, I saw several listings including one at $5-million. Now keep in mind I *didn't have $5-million; heck, I didn't have much more than 5 cents in my pocket, and just kind of ignored that listing when I first saw it. I kept looking and noticed that same listing a few more times over the next several weeks.*

One day I got a call from an agent I'd been networking with, and he brought me this same $5-million deal, saying it was financially distressed and the Owner had to sell. We discussed the details. Turns out that an over-priced management company had been doing something crazy. Paying themselves first, they used the remaining net cash flow to pay expenses until the money ran out each month, and then put the rest of the invoices in a drawer, unpaid.

This went on for months and months until nearly 2 years had passed and the unpaid vendor invoices totaled over $50,000! By that time, the vendors had stopped providing services, the property was suffering from deferred maintenance, vacancies were rising and cash flow was falling. The management company finally went to the owner to let him know there was a problem, and that he needed to pay $50,000 to resolve it.

The out-of-town absentee Owner, who was financially strapped and had already listed the property for sale, was unable to pay. He called the agent and said, "Sell Now, whatever it takes." That's a motivated seller.

So I put my mind to thinking how I could structure a deal. Analyzing the financials, I saw that if I fired the management company and managed the property myself, cash flow could cover the repairs needed to lease up the vacant units, and provide a nice profit after that.

We proposed a Master Lease Purchase Option. In the Master Lease offer we stipulated that we'd use cash flow to send him a lease payment that would cover his mortgage, taxes and insurance each month. We'd also cover all expenses going forward and handle all operations, along with an option to purchase in 4 years.

Owner came back wanting a $75,000 down payment and 90-10 split of net positive cash flow (10% to us). We countered with $25,000 down, take over the $50,000 of unpaid invoices, and agreed to a 50-50 split.

For the Purchase Option we agreed to pay Seller's list price. Done; we had our deal.

Then I had to figure out how to pay for it, since I had no money. Contacting private lending sources, I ultimately found one who gave me a signature loan for $25,000 at 12% with a two year term. That's how I acquired my $5-million property with no money out of pocket.

Regards,
Bill

There's a little more to Bill's story. Yes, he got the deal done with none of his own money, but it took a lot of work, strategic negotiations, and personal sacrifice. In fact, he structured his 12% private loan payment to be paid off within the required two years, and then made a tidy profit over the following two years.

He started by working his tail off, personally cleaning units, and improving the property overall, as well as paying contractors for repairs. By increasing rents each year, he also increased the property value and equity.

So let's dig a little deeper and see what we can learn from how he structured this deal, and how he made it happen.

Through learning the lessons that Bill learned, you, too, can structure a great deal! He had another problem at the outset: no vendors or contractors would work on the property to do the repairs until they were paid what was owed them... remember that $50,000?

How did he handle that $50,000 debt? He got even more creative and came up with some very strategic negotiations. Bill told the vendors he'd really like to work with them, and gave them two options: (1) to take pennies on the dollar for what they were owed, or (2) to receive an exclusive contract to service his property for 4 years, *if* they'd release him from their past due collection claims.

At this point, enough time had elapsed that the vendors and contractors couldn't place liens against the property, so they didn't have a lot of options. Neither did Bill. Not all the contractors agreed at first, but several did, so Bill was able to get enough of the needed repairs done to lease the down units, fix the deferred maintenance issues, and to increase rents. While this negotiation wasn't quite as easy as it sounds, it worked.

But Bill still had another problem: he also needed to make his monthly payments on time, and pay for utility and other expenses, in addition to paying for repairs. He set up a strict budget to allocate cash flow: first to his monthly payments on the signature loan, then to the lease payments owed the seller, then to expenses, and finally to accomplish repairs. Things were tight, and with significant personal sacrifice, he made it. As he was able to increase rents and generate additional cash flow, he was able to pay off his loan, pay expenses, pay the vendors, pay the seller, and finally earn himself a decent paycheck, too.

Bill's is a great story of creativity, hard word, sacrifice, and getting a difficult deal done. Profitably. One of the most powerful things he did was to negotiate that $50,000 debt down to pennies on the dollar. You can negotiate expenses with contractors and vendors, especially when they want your business.

You may be able to find hidden funds by negotiating for installment payments over time instead of paying up front. You can partner with them, too, by giving them an equity stake in exchange for renovating down units.

And you'd be surprised what 'extra' leverage you can negotiate with Contractors, Vendors, Renters, Realtors, Agents, Brokers, and others, to help you preserve cash, reduce expenses, or obtain needed funds.

Category C: Extra Leverage – where Buyer can leverage outside or 'extra' funding sources

What follows are several strategies that leverage outside or 'extra' sources that can help fund your deal. In my opinion, no potential resource for funding or helping to fund a deal should be overlooked. In that spirit, I share with you five 'extra' sources you can consider as you seek to uncover money to fund your deals. I've used each one of these strategies to great effect, and several times I've combined one or more with another strategy. I hope you can envision using these strategies to your advantage.

17.**Contractors & Vendors** – where a Buyer negotiates favorable prices or payment terms

Where repairs are needed upon acquisition of a property, the name of the game is to make cash king… utilize cash flow wherever possible to pay for essential repairs. When you receive estimates for needed work, remember that everything is negotiable. A Buyer or New Owner may be able to negotiate with each Contractor or supplies Vendor to:

(a) reduce price based on granting an exclusivity privilege, where that contractor will be the only one in his trade allowed on site for a specified number of years; or

(b) accept a small percentage of property equity in exchange for doing substantial work to make down unit(s) inhabitable and rentable (and thereby generate increased cash flow); or

(c) accept as payment for work completed, a specified percentage of net positive cash-flow for a specified period of time, thus eliminating up-front capital outlay; or

(d) accept payment terms (extend credit) that allow Buyer or New Owner the ability to pay for work completed in payment installments over several months, rather than all up front.

Some contractors simply won't be able to eliminate 100% of upfront costs, as they have to purchase supplies, pay wages, etc.

The point is, based on your needs, you can ask, propose and negotiate everything, and you won't know the answer until you actually ask.

18. Renters or Tenants– where funds supplied by Renters can be leveraged to Buyer advantage

Considering that every multi-family property has renters, there are several ways to leverage funds supplied by tenants during the normal course of business operations. This strategy works especially well with long-term renters, and can be combined with #17 above: Contractors.

(a) Tenant security deposits and pro-rationed monthly rents can be used as credits in closing, reducing cash outlay at closing, or increasing cash distributions from escrow to Buyer.

(b) Buyer/New Owner can often reach a deal with a tenant in what I call an "Upgrade Opportunity Session." When you acquire a property, ask tenants for their wish list of repairs and apartment upgrades like carpet, flooring, kitchen, bathroom, or appliances. The Buyer/New Owner directs the property manager to acknowledge each Tenant's list, cite the costs to upgrade, and negotiate a rent increase based on mutually agreed upgrades to be completed. Then a new lease with higher rent is signed, upgrades are completed, and property value immediately appreciates along with cash flow.

(c) Since the tenants actually participate in the rent increase decision (due to desired upgrades, some of which have to be done anyway), they feel like the building owners truly care about them, and tenant morale also increases, which can result in referrals of like-minded tenants as vacancies need to be filled.

As an Owner, I always treat tenants as "residents" – good residents represent the gold in my apartment treasure chest, and I treat them like the gold they are.

19.Realtors, Agents, Brokers – where the Broker relationship is leveraged to seal a deal

In a particularly tight or protracted negotiation, or facing an impasse situation with a Seller,

(a) As a Buyer, You can negotiate with the Buyer's broker, and the Seller's broker, to consider a commission reduction in order to close the deal, and they may concede. In some cases the broker may even make the suggestion, just to get the deal closed. Commission reduction must be used as an exception, only in rare circumstances, or you may find that brokers will know your name and not want to work with you. Realtors work hard for their commissions and deserve to be paid.

(b) As a Seller, or Buyer, you can negotiate with brokers to carry a Promissory Note to pay their full commission over time, instead of Brokers receiving cash at close of escrow. This reduces the cash outlay at closing, or can increase cash distributions from escrow to the Buyer.

(c) Also, Realtors themselves are often investors, and know other investors, so it can be very productive to invite them to lunch and talk about investing in your deals in connection with #11 above: Investors and Sponsors.

20.Transactional Funding – where a closing-period loan is made to facilitate a double closing

Transactional funding, using third party funds, may be used to facilitate a purchase transaction, usually involving a property flip or series of two buyers closing at the same time (double close).

For example, Initial Seller 'A' goes under contract with initial Buyer 'B,' who is typically a wholesaler we'll call Buyer/Seller 'B', and Buyer/Seller 'B' already has a Buyer 'C' lined up to Buy from 'B' at a higher price. Transactional funding is the closing-period loan (usually 1-3 days, but sometimes several days) made purely to finance the transaction from A to B above, allowing the final sale and transfer of title from B to C above.

While not used frequently in multi-family deals, Transactional Funding deals are sometimes used with certain off-market deals where there is ample profit to be had between the price points of a double transaction sale, where Buyer/Seller B needs no funds out of pocket, but can make a profit by going under contract first with Seller A, to ultimately sell to Buyer C.

Sometimes Buyer/Seller B obtains super-short-term Transaction Funding to acquire the property for a few days or weeks to make some low-cost cosmetic improvements, thus lengthening the closing period required to close the sale transaction to ultimate Buyer C.

Transactional Funding simply facilitates the transfer of title from A, through B, to C, the ultimate Buyer. Often no outside funding is needed at all, but there are certain times Buyer B actually must close with funds in escrow and therefore must obtain a super-short-term transactional loan, where funds are borrowed, deposited into escrow, and then paid back upon final closing (Seller B to Buyer C).

21.Retirement plans – where retirement funds are used to invest in real estate deals

Although brokerage houses and banks have been known to say that retirement funds like 401k plans, Traditional IRAs or Roth IRAs cannot be used to invest in real estate, the truth is that banks and brokerage houses are simply not structured to facilitate such investments.

Retirement funds such as 401k plans have provisions for loans. Both Traditional and Roth IRAs can, in fact, be used for direct investment in real estate, as long as certain rules are followed and there is no "self-dealing" (e.g., buying from or selling to family members).

(a) Many retirement accounts allow loans at low interest rates, and these loan proceeds may be used to make a down payment or investment in a property. Be cautious when contemplating retirement plan loans, as certain loans may become due and payable in full if you lose your job, leave your job, or get a new job; know your plan before executing a retirement loan.

(b) Traditional IRAs or Roth IRAs can be structured as "Self-Directed" IRAs, and funds may then be directed to purchase income properties, as long as the transaction is compliant with IRS rules (e.g., self-dealing). NOTE: Income derived from an IRA-wholly-owned property may only be received by the IRA, and not directly received by an individual.

(c) "Self-Dealing:" Your IRA may not buy an investment from, nor sell an investment to, a disqualified person as defined by Internal Revenue Code Section 4975, essentially meaning family members. To do so is known as "self-dealing" and is not allowed.

(d) Additionally, investments made with self-directed IRA funds must be at "arm's length," which is defined as a willing buyer and willing seller coming together with no undue influence from outside sources.

(e) Monies in Self-directed IRAs can be invested in your own real estate deals, or in other peoples' deals, instead of being invested in stock market shares or mutual funds. NOTE that Self-directed IRA funds must be in a Custodial Account held by a knowledgeable financial firm in order to facilitate real estate investments; typical banks and brokerage firms do not trade outside the traditional stock market, and hence cannot facilitate real estate deals. You may search online to find references for Self-Directed IRA or Custodial firms.

Retirement Plans are a great source of funds to make your own account funds work harder for you, or to provide opportunities for earning higher returns to others: business associates, investors, relatives, friends, potential equity and debt partners.

Always talk about solid returns people can receive from real estate deals, safely secured by real estate assets that are actively and profitably producing positive cash flow. Returns from real estate are far higher than what retirement plan funds are earning at the bank, guaranteed!

Crowd Funding – Online fund sourcing is now a reality

Watch out world, here comes a new era seeking to democratize the world of venture capital. Now the "little guy" can participate in big projects. The idea of crowd funding a real estate project has been in the minds of real estate entrepreneurs for years, but it's been widely considered more of a dream than a reality.

Since 2012, several groups have formed to create so-called Crowd Funding websites, but these are primarily online Marketing channels that are raising money from accredited investors using syndications, joint ventures, and methods that have been around for decades. Nevertheless, these new firms or "web portals" have positioned themselves to take full advantage of online fund sourcing as new SEC rules are implemented.

In the past, due to regulatory laws and the fact that only a few high net-worth individuals could qualify as "accredited investors" under SEC rules, raising capital effectively reduced the crowd to a VIP short list. For years, real estate investors have utilized partnering syndication via Private Placement Memoranda, under Regulation D allowing accredited investors to participate in deals. And to date, crowd funding and rules surrounding its use have been more like a nightmare than a dream.

However, New Rules for Title IV of the JOBS act, announced March 25, 2015, and the crowd funding dream has become very real. Congress negotiated a clever way to cut the red tape and finally allow the non-accredited, average investor to have an active seat at the negotiating table via crowd funding.

Okay, so there are rules to obey, and procedures to follow, but the unaccredited "little guy" can now participate as an investor. We'll get into those rules, but first let's review the background.

While "accredited" investors must have greater than $1 million net worth, or earn more than $200,000 per year,(or $300,000 jointly with spouse), and certify their financial accreditation with the SEC, the "non-accredited" investor will simply have to declare (a) personal income (verified by most recent Tax Return), and (b) personal net worth (verified by unaudited Personal Financial Statement), and (c) may make investments up to ten percent (10%) of verified income or declared net worth.

This 10% limitation imposed by the SEC is to "protect" the consumer, and only applies to Tier II investing (explained below).

Now that unaccredited investors are able to invest in projects, real estate entrepreneurs can start raising capital via online crowd funding. Let's say, for example, you are sponsoring a deal to acquire a 200-unit multifamily property with a repositioning opportunity; how would you achieve that using crowd funding? My friend and Phoenix real estate broker, Bob Collopy, outlines the steps below.

Step 1. You start by finding an online intermediary that has a "funding portal" approved by FINRA (Financial Industry

Regulatory Authority), which licenses participants, reviews regulatory compliance, and works with the SEC. There are a number of web-based portals already operating, and each has their own systems, guidelines, and objectives.

You will have to research and interview these intermediary funding portals, and their fee structures, to find a good fit for you and your project. You will then use their methods and procedures for getting your project online to raise funds, and to ensure your project is fully compliant with FINRA and the SEC.

How do you ensure your crowd funding project is fully compliant with the SEC?

Step 2. To answer this question you have to determine which government approved method of crowd funding you will use. This is not as difficult as it sounds, but we're going to present the rules, which are not as complicated as they look. There's still a downside for real estate investment utilizing crowd funding, but at least there are rules that allow testing the waters.

Currently, there are four methods available to use crowd funding, but only two worth considering for the crowd: (1) Regulation D, (2) Regulation CF, and the two new Regulation A options: (3) Tier I, and (4) Tier II. Regulation D only allows accredited investors, so we won't discuss that any further. Regulation CF is another method we won't discuss because its rules are so strict that it is borderline useless. The real leap forward with the 2015 Announcement is Regulation A+: the availability of Tier I and Tier II options for crowd funding.

The Tier I option allows one to raise up to $20 million (maximum), has fewer regulatory and accounting rules, but requires state-by-state approval for each state in which one desires to raise capital.

For smaller, in-state projects, this may be a welcome rule. Even for a regional or nation-wide capital raise, obtaining approval is now simplified via "Coordinated Review" to be handled by the new (as yet untested) North American Securities Administrators Association (NASAA) program, which is a cooperative between the states to get approval on crowd funding more quickly.

While regulatory scrutiny is more flexible (e.g., project financials are merely reviewed, not audited), another advantage is that the non-accredited investor has no limits on the amount that may be invested (not subject to the 10% of income/assets rule).

One downside with Tier 1 is the question of how well the Coordinated Review will work among the States, how long and how complicated the approval process could become. Time will tell.

Another downside risk is that States will retain full enforcement and anti-fraud jurisdiction in all cases, which means that an organization could be subject to 50 different State's rules and interpretations. Costs could be astronomical should investor complaints or law suits be filed, with or without cause. For these reasons, most experts agree that the Tier II option will become more popular than Tier I, under the new Regulation A+.

The Tier II option is like a mini-IPO and is expected to become popular and widely used because one can raise up to $50 million (maximum), and it does not require State-by-State approvals, but only requires approval from the SEC to raise capital nationwide.

This is important because former rules severely limited a capital raise; the new limit has been raised to $50 million. This stunning maneuver by Congress creates a new rule that trumps state approvals, and eliminate all those extra state filing fees.

This SEC pre-emption over state-by-state regulation is the single most important advantage that allows crowd funding to open doors to the average investor.

One perceived downside to Tier II is that project financials are required to be audited and certified annually, but that, frankly, makes good business sense. It's also possible that tax records of both the project and the investors may receive greater scrutiny and be monitored on an ongoing basis. Finally, the "non-accredited" investor is limited to investing a maximum of ten percent (10%) of verified income or declared net worth; this limit is imposed for investor and consumer protection.

Step 3. After selecting your intermediary funding portal, and choosing which government program you'll use, you'll prepare a business plan in order to complete an Offering Circular.

Offering Circular Approval is Required: The issuer will need to file a disclosure document and audited financials with the SEC. The SEC must approve the document prior to any sales. The proposed rule indicates that the Offering Circular will receive the same level of scrutiny as a Form S-1 in an IPO. *This may be the biggest potential drawback of using Regulation A+ and may limit crowd funding to larger organizations, as opposed to the real estate entrepreneur. But the web portal firms may mitigate this concern through their methods and procedures established to allow smaller size projects to be funded via their crowdfunding sites*

Once your Offering Circular is approved, your project is up and running on the crowd funding portal, and you're on your way to actually funding the project!

Step 4. Regulation A+ allows advertising. There is no general solicitation restriction so you can publicly advertise and discuss your offering, including at meet-ups, seminars, radio, television, and via social media. However, one thing you cannot do is get an endorsement from the website company that is supplying the funding portal for your project, for example.

Thanks to Title IV New Rules, you can now advertise your capital-raising project on almost any medium!

And there you have it: I want to thank my friend and real estate broker, Bob Collopy, for outlining the four steps required to get your project ready for Crowd Funding.

Fad or Reality?

"Crowd Funding" is so named because it allows a project to be financed by a large pool of investors, who can each contribute a small amount toward an acquisition or development.

Crowd funding takes place on a web-based platform, or funding portal, allowing users to reach a huge number of potential contributors.

Unlike the traditional development model, which requires a large amount of capital up front, crowdfunding has a low-capital entry requirement (often allowing pledges of $1000 or less), and gives investors greater control over which business endeavors or projects get funded.

Previously, the only other option for the small-capital real estate investor was to invest in a Real Estate Investment Trust (often shorthanded to "REIT"). Purchasing a share in a REIT allows an investor to buy into a professionally managed portfolio of existing properties. REITs offer only indirect ownership, however, and can have relatively high fees.

In contrast, crowd funding offers investors the opportunity to select specific projects with no fees, rather than a portfolio with hefty management fees. The crowd funding process is conceptually more transparent in that investment results are posted on the Internet as the project progresses. It's too soon to tell whether crowd funding is merely a fad or whether we'll see a change in the way real estate projects are funded. Stay tuned.

CONCLUSION

We've presented and discussed 21 exciting and workable ways to find hidden sources of money to fund your projects, and introduced crowd funding as a possible new way to find contributors for your profitable deals in the future.

Use these techniques to create wealth and find untold millions to develop your projects and acquisitions. Do it one project at a time. Take action.

Remember: The true essence of every good real estate deal lies in the structure of the deal acquisition itself: how you structure your purchase of a property asset. Your purchase price, more than any other single factor, will determine how profitable the deal can become. Understanding where value can be added is vital. Identifying your exit strategy is also key, and believe it or not, planning how and when you'll exit a deal, can help you better structure your purchase and acquisition in the first place.

That "Green light" Feeling

I remember driving to an appointment at the far end of Broadway in the city of Oakland, California some years ago. I got off the freeway and onto this major street through the center of town, stretching from Claremont and North Oakland all the way down to Jack London square at the waterfront. It was early in the morning, just turning daylight, and it seemed like I was the only one on that broad street.

There was no other traffic, but the red light was taking forever to change. Finally it turned green and before you knew it, I faced another traffic light in front of me. It was red, and just as I started stepping on my brakes, the light turned green.

Taking in the view down that long street, it looked like Christmas, seeing intersections for miles in front of me, some lights green, some yellow, some red; lights flashing and changing colors at different intervals.

Approaching the next intersection, the light turned green. I smiled. Coming up to the next street, the light turned green again. I looked at my speed, 25 mph, so I kept it right at 25. Next intersection: the light turned green. Next street: green again.

I started to feel like God was smiling down on me, turning all the lights green, just for me.

Have you ever had that feeling? It made me grin from ear to ear. I was beaming. It made me laugh. Out loud. It made me happy. It made me start singing, rocking out, drumming the steering wheel. It actually thrilled me that I drove for miles, intersection after intersection, and every single light turned green right when I got there. It felt like the world was open for business, and I was the VIP Preferred Customer; I'd won the prize; leave your wallet at home!

Friends, I have never been able to repeat that experience, but I still cherish that feeling. I feel that same "green light" feeling when I put together a real estate deal where everything seems to come together. A deal that pleases the seller. A deal that pleases me. A deal that pleases my contributors; a deal that leaves my wallet at home.

May you enjoy that green light feeling as you go out and do your next deal? Here's to you... You've gotten a green light; Go and find your hidden millions!

Questions? Need a sponsor, investor, or partner for a Multi-Family Residential property acquisition? Pick up the phone or email us today. If we can't help you achieve your dreams, then we're committed to helping you figure out who can. Our promise to you is that it will be the best, most meaningful phone call you have ever made.

Tel: 877-702-3863
Email: Lane@YourHiddenMillions.com
Visit us www.YourHiddenMillions.com

Self Storage Facilities, The Fastest and Easiest Way to Make Money in Commercial Real Estate

Jeff Lindahl

Let me give you an overview on how I got started. Have you been to the Boston Fish Pier? Across the street from the No Name restaurants, Bart Truman's Fisheries had a sign saying "Everyone shovels their own Ice except for Mabel". Mabel was a legend on the pier, she was also my grandmother.

My grandfather died at the age of forty-two and left Mabel with four teenage girls, a son age two and a newly opened fish market. They all worked there to survive, my Mom learned how to cut fish. Mabel grew it into a success business because we gave quantity and quality. Who likes quantity and quality? I do, that was the way I was raised.

We all worked there: my Mom, my two brothers, my sister, my twenty cousins and all of my aunts--everyone except my Uncle Fred. He wanted to frame houses with my uncle Bob. Mabel would not allow anyone to move out of Abington, except for Fred. He moved to upper state New York working as a women's clothes sales rep. Fred was only eight years older than us cousins.

I was the second oldest cousin. I had hands-on experience and the fish market was mine to take over at the age of seventeen (especially when my fried seafood plate was voted the Best in Boston by the Boston Globe newspaper). Well, something happened that changed my future. Anyone have something that changed your future? Well, Fred wanted "IN" and Mabel handed the fish market over to him. So, I had a big decision to make. I could work for Fred or I could move on.

Growing up in my small town, I knew I would eventually own a business. On the main block of North Avenue in Abington, my grandmother owned a fish market, my uncle owned Bud's gas station & repair shop and, most importantly, my aunt's brother-in-law owned Owens's News (the candy store).

My uncle Bob owned a good sized house framing company. My business was with my brother Dave, we had a great newspaper route. We also shoveled a lot of snow in the day. That's when I learned to delegate. We hired Gerhardt, our next door neighbor. He was as strong as an ox, but more importantly, he knew how to negotiate. We would look at a driveway and tell Gerhardt to go to the door and get us forty dollars and he would. He was three years younger than us! So, back to my big decision.

I decided to go to College at Northeastern in Boston. They had a 5-year plan where you work some semesters. I really wanted to be a lawyer but I saw that one of the Kennedys was having a hard time passing the bar. Imagine going to college for five years and then not passing. What do you fall back on? So I created a plan. I would give engineering a shot, and if that did not work I would try accounting. I enrolled into the engineering program to see if I could do it because I had heard that engineers make a lot of money. I was sitting in my first class and the instructor said, "look to the person on your right, and look at the person on your left. Only one of you will be here next year because that person will want to succeed."

LOOK TO YOUR RIGHT AND LOOK TO YOUR LEFT. YOU ALL WILL SUCCEED BECAUSE I AM GOING TO SHARE WITH YOU A TON OF INFORMATION ABOUT INVESTING IN SELF STORAGE !!!!

Hey, I struggled during my first semester. I noticed 2 guys pulling great grades. I found out that they belonged to a fraternity, an engineering fraternity. Do you know what I Did? Yes, I joined that fraternity, more importantly, I surrounded myself with "like-minded people.

I GRADUATED with BSME. More importantly, the real estate seed was planted. One of our alumni, Ed Knuckle, was working 6 months at a time as an engineer on the oil rig in Saudi Arabia. He would return after six months and we would have the pledges roll out the red carpet for him as he was walking off the plane. We did it because he was an alumni coming home to stay with us at the frat. Ed started buying brownstones on Commonwealth Avenue in the mid 1980's with the chunks of money that he had made. That's what I wanted to do.

Engineering went well and after a few years I got recruited by two of our competitors, one was two towns away from Abington and the other on the coast near New Hampshire, and they made me a great offer. I moved out of Abington to the northern coast.

I got my first experience as a land developer. I bought a raw five acre lot and became the general contractor and I turned the dirt into my dream house -- for dirt-cheap money.

This is my wife Joan, my daughters Colette and Shannon and my son Jonathan.

Joan and I grew up a few blocks away from each other. She has nine brothers and sisters. When I say I am a big family guy, you will know that I am a big family guy with a BIG family. Things were good until Colette was born and I realized that she would not be growing up with her cousins. The whole time that I was working on the northern coast company, the other company was always in constant contact with me about taking their offer. They knew me better than I thought.

I put my house on the market and we moved back to Joan's mother's house with her mother Jeanne. It's was great for six months, then the guy running the place where I worked went off his meds (I did not even know he was on meds) and they closed the place. I got laid off. I started looking for a job. While I was looking, my brother ask me if I wanted to do some landscaping for the company that he had just started until I found a new job or got called back.

So now I am laid off, living at my mother in-law's house with wife Joan and daughter Colette. Our house in Georgetown, which was fifty miles away, was on the market and life was crazy. My brother Dave gave me a great opportunity.

He gave me a part-time job planting flowers and pulling weeds for his new landscape company while I looked for a full time job. You know, we have always heard that when the window of opportunity opens up you jump through, but you never realize it until you have lost a few times. So Dave tells me that one of the guys at the gym is a real estate broker that has contractors put bids on Fannie Mae foreclosures in Brockton, and he wants to show him how to do it.

Great! I watch as Dave pulls in my Dad, who is a jack of all trades, to help with the bids and the repairs. He does a few and Fannie Mae is very pleased and makes him an official

Fannie Mae contractor. There are three others in our region. Now he can bid twenty properties a week.

Being an engineer I knew that we needed a system for bidding repairs and a way to pull our own permits. Uncle Bob would pull ours. So, I found a Certified Repair Estimation Course and a prep course to taking the Massachusetts's Contractor's License Courses.

I completed both and soon I was running a fifteen man rehab construction crew. I learned how to put a house back together and how to hire and run the people to do it quality. We did a few houses, the bank liked it, and soon we were doing hundreds of them. Then I started realizing that people were investing these. They were buying them and selling them and flipping them.

I wanted to do that. I asked the investors all kinds of questions. Then I went through the Carlton Sheets course and flew down to Orlando to attend a Ron LaGrande course. I then started attending REIA clubs. I met people that were just starting out and experienced investors.

Then we started buying these from Fannie Mae and taking the money to invest in 3-families. I started buying 3-families and 6-families, we just kept buying properties. Soon the real estate market started to change. There was a lot of job growth in our area. The inventory of Fannie Mae Properties dried up.

So we had to decide what to do next. We were going to open two businesses, a real estate office and an exterminating company. I would do both. I would learn all I could about the exterminating business and then be able to hire people to do it; I would also work as a real estate agent. Well, the exterminating company fizzled out because of the high risk and liability insurance.

So, I concentrated on working as a real estate agent. Then I saw another opportunity. I figured that I could make more money with multifamily than with residential because the commission is based on the purchase price. I was still a very active investor and I did not want to drive around with buyers all weekend. So I bought a list of multifamily owners and started direct mailing to them. In the letter I indicated to them that I would teach them how to do a 1031 Exchange to avoid capital gains.

I became one of the Top Real Estate Agents in Brockton. I specialized in multifamily. I would tell the seller that I could buy his property. If it was not a sweet deal then at the end of the conversation I would tell them how I could list it, get it sold and possibly get them into another property with their 1031 Exchange. Thus, I was building my private money investor list.

This worked out great for a few years, then the market peaked and became a seller's market. My property had more than tripled in price. Dave then told me about a company that was bringing him to look at properties in Mississippi. It was the start of moving out of our local market into new markets across the United States.

We were going to move up from small multis into large apartment complexes. I needed to know everything that I could about them. I treated it as a new business. I created systems and checklists to verify that the deal that was presented to me was actually the deal that I was buying. The real estate club that we were going to was kind of shady so we started our own. That's when we started educating investors on what we were doing. I figured that if I could educate them then it would reduce the risk that they felt about being a partner or just going out to do their own deal. I also learned a lot from them. I would bounce a lot of ideas.

One of the best ideas was looking at ways to increase the revenue that a property could bring and how to decrease operating expenses. I looked at renting rooms, creating sober houses, charging tenants for water, renter's insurance, and converting basements into apartments (not a good idea).

My First Self Storage Units

I had just bought a 3-family with a 3-bay garage. I usually padlock the cellar and the garages at my properties. This keeps tenants from putting things down there and moving out and leaving it. It also stops the drug activity. I hired a contractor to put on a new rubber roof. He did a lot of work in the area. He told me that he would fix the roof on the garage for free if he could rent out two of the bays. "It's a deal," I told him. So I created individual leases for each garage bay.

Look at the revenues that I created:

3 units x $50 = $150 per month additional Cash Flow.

If the average Cash Flow for a 3-family is $600 per month, I have just increased my Cash Flow to $750 or by 25 %.

This was actually the property that I would sell, as the market was peaking, for a nice profit to move into an apartment complex.

A few years later we are heavy into investing in Emerging Markets. The thing about analyzing the numbers is that it's all about the story that they are telling you. If a deal looks like it could be good, I will run the numbers and take notes on what my take is on them. Dave will do it, or someone else from our acquisition team. So we are very strong at running the numbers.

Then, we will fly down as a team and one group will do the unit-by-unit inspection while the other team is in the leasing office pulling leases and conducting the lease audit. So, I see in the back corner of the property, just off the parking lot in a irregular shape lot, are some self storage units.

What a great idea! They just poured a cement pad and dropped and hooked prefabricated units. I did not see a specific "Storage Income" figure just an "Other Income" value, and there wasn't any "Storage Operating Expense" itemized. So, I grabbed the property manager to give me the numbers. She told me that there were 60 units. The tenants were renting them at $70 per month and there has been a waiting list. So I asked her what the operating expenses were. She said that she may spend a few minutes each month on average with the billing, and may change a light bulb every now and then.

I am thinking that's Hidden Cash Flow,
60 units x $70 = $4200

$4200 x 12 months = $50,400

Value = $50,400/ 9.5 Cap = $530,536

I added Self Storage Investing to my business model and YOU
    should too!

60 units x $70 = $4200 Who would like that in their pockets?

I am thinking that looking for irregular shaped lots in an apartment complex is like buying a 3-family with a garage. I could ask for a repair allowance to pay for the pad and the units. I added Self Storage Investing to my business model and YOU should too! Do you know that most successful Real Estate Investors have added self storage to their portfolio?

Did you know that Warren Buffet is one of the largest Self Storage owners in the United States? Warren Buffet - **"Self-storage companies seem to be the 'Cinderella segment' of commercial real estate in a faltering economy."** Oh, If Warren Buffett is in, DO YOU THINK it is a good deal?

Investors love self storage for many reasons. One of the more important reasons is the reduced management role. Self storage requires less management than residential rentals. All management is required to do is rent units and collect the rent. Managers do not have to paint, replace carpet, unstop toilets or worry about collecting the rent or having to evict a tenant. They can sleep knowing they will not have to provide a tenant with a new key or anything else.

Hey, this is the great thing about self storage--it's becoming automated. A kiosk actually rents to tenants; they come to the kiosk, they can see what units are available and they can see what the pricing is. There are so many ways to increase your revenues. Here are some of the value Plays: Future Expansion, Bill Boards, Cell Tower, RV and Boat Storage.

Be a transactional engineer, be able to take down any deal that comes across your plate. A lot of times I am direct mailing to apartment complexes that tell about other types of properties that they have for sale at the right price such as office buildings, strip malls, marinas, etc. Also, real estate brokers will know when sellers want to sell different types of properties. Well that is what happened to us. Our Dallas broker called us about a self storage facility that two partners needed to sell. It was the final piece of a 1031 Exchange that they were putting together to take down a bigger project. Lucky me, I was assigned the task of doing the due diligence of the self storage business--what makes a good property financially, what makes a good self storage market and then, why is this a good property in this location in this market. We did not want to get into a bad deal, especially with our investors. That was my new mission.

The deal was an 872-unit in Pasadena, TX. We took it over at 75% occupancy because that had just finished Phase 4 and there were no lease ups. So, I analyzed it on today's numbers, the Actual Numbers. We determined a great discount price of $8 million. I love working with motivated sellers. I projected that when it was filled at 90%, it would be worth $10 Million dollars. In my research, I discovered that Self Storage takes a while to lease up BUT once it is leased up it stays there. I figured that Phase 4 would take a year or two to do it, to reach the $10 Million mark. Who would be interested in investing in a self storage facility and have the management company lease it up and in 2 years be worth 2 MILLION DOLLARS? ANYBODY ?

This is the information that blew my mind. HERE IS THE THING, a hurricane came through. Do you think that was good or bad? It was bad for everyone else, but we happened to be on a hill. We were the only dry self storage facility in the area. We went from 70% to 88% in 5 months. We made the $10 Million mark. Thank you Mother Nature!

Are you familiar with Ben Stein? He was on the commercial with Shaq. You know that he is a genius don't you? The guy is a financial genius. He has been a millionaire many, many times over. He's got his own show. He has other people following him. Check out what he has to say.

"I can't think of one single long term trend in our country and our economy that doesn't benefit Self Storage. It's the perfect storm--a hurricane of Profits. This is the sweetest spot in the whole American economy, a receptacle for an enormous cascade of money"

We are in the Best of Times. We are in a time of transition, and that makes a perfect storm for investing in self storage facilities. Why are we in a perfect storm? We've got the Economy, we've got baby boomers and we've got Echo Boomers. Let me explain. The Economy, it is on the recovery road but the banks are going to release more foreclosures, which will force people to put their stuff into storage. Baby Boomers, the baby boomer generation, everyone that uses self storage is a Baby Boomer, they are getting old now.

They are downsizing. They collected a lot of things over the years, things that they don't want to part with, heirlooms. The Consumer Age, and they consumed and consumed and bought. 73 million and they are putting it all into self storage. And you've got the Echo Boomers, 72 million Echo Boomers coming into the marketplace. They were taught to over buy and to put their old stuff into storage. And that is why we are a self storage nation . That is why self storage is just going to continue to grow in value year after year after year.

Self storage offers a **HIGHER RETURN ON INVESTMENT** with a comparably lower failure rate than many other real estate ventures or new businesses. Self storage allows you to **START**

SMALL AND GROW OVER TIME. **Self storage demand** is driven by life events: downsizing homes, job transfers, divorce. Additionally, many businesses opt to outsource storage needs. The time is now to buy a self storage facility and BUILD A SOLID BUSINESS. The NEED FOR COMMERCIAL USE IS GROWING. More people are also becoming at-home entrepreneurs and seek alternative storage other than their home or garage. 1 in 10 Households Need or Use Self Storage

IT'S EASILY MANAGED. As a low cost investment, Self Storage can easily be managed by individuals with little or no experience. The initial investment is much smaller and operating expenses are much lower than other types of real estate investments. The management task, unlike many other businesses, is not labor intensive. Best of all, **No Jerry Springer Tenants, No Toilets, No Trash, and NO PAIN. The Self Storage Make Ready Procedure** - open the unit's door, walk to the rear and pull the gas powered leaf blower. Make Readies are done in minutes.

SELF STORAGE IS A MONEY MAKER WITHOUT THE HEADACHES. Over 40% of commercial customers rent for more than two years. The average customer visits his unit once a month. Real estate properties must continually maintain grounds, appliances, plumbing, electrical fixtures, etc., which usually require a maintenance staff. Self Storage operating costs are a fraction of other real estate properties.

BREAK-EVEN OCCUPANCY RATES. WHEN you own a rental property, you must rent a certain amount of space to be profitable. In self storage, the break-even point is considerably lower than other real estate ventures. Break Even Occupancy

Comparison for Self Storage is 60-72%, All other Real Estate, it's 80-90%.

So how do we get paid with self-storage? Well, we're going to get paid three different ways. We're going to get paid through Cash Flow. The Cash Flow is the money that we get from our property on a regular basis. We're going to get paid through Appreciation. Appreciation is the money that we're going to get from raising our rents, so always be raising the rents by $10 or $20. It's called a nuisance increase. And the reason it's called a nuisance increase is because it's a nuisance that they get it, but it's not high enough that they're going to go move their stuff into another facility.

And then number three, and my favorite way, is what's called Acquisition Fees. It's industry standard. You take the time to discover and educate yourself on how to get these storage deals, and you also take the time to discover how to get the private money for these storage deals (the people that will give you the money). Then, it's customary in our business, and your business as well because we're in the same business, that you get an Acquisition Fee.

And an Acquisition Fee is anywhere between 1% and 5% of the purchase price paid at the closing by the investors. And that's a beautiful thing because not only do you get in with no money out of your pocket but they actually pay you at the closing! And they're happy to pay you because the investors are focused on their returns, and as long as you're giving them a certain return you will be able to get the Acquisition Fees. So, that's a good thing.

Failure Rate Comparison:

* Self storage maintains value during both good and bad economic times.

* Failure Rate: Office/Retail 60%

* Self Storage: 8%

* Lenders Lend on IT. Do you want to be part of the 60% club or the 8%????

So, who's renting from us now? Who's renting the space in our storage facilities? Well, I mentioned foreclosed homeowners, but also apartment dwellers. One of the best places to own a storage facility is right next to a large apartment complex, or right in the middle of what we like to call apartment row where there's a lot of apartments right in a row in any particular city.

Also, college students that are going off to college, and all of a sudden they find themselves in a very small dorm room. They know they're going to be there may be their first year but not their second. Well, they move a lot of stuff into storage while they're there in anticipation of moving out.

Unfortunately, 50% of Americans get divorced. So, when there's a divorce, typically the person that moves out moves into an apartment and their stuff is moved into storage. Also, landscapers, contractors, anybody in the trades are always looking for storage facilities. Home sellers that have too much stuff as they're selling their houses; they'll go into storage facilities. Boomers downsizing and homebuyers going into new housing that may be not the right size for all of their stuff. But also, another great place to own storage facilities is outside 55 and older communities. There are communities now where you have to be 55 years or older to live there.

New developments are also a great place for storage because you have people moving into the new development, and storage facilities do well there also.

Now, there are different ways that you can get the deal. You can get deals from direct mail, sending out letters and post cards to owners of storage facilities. You can get deals from Real Estate brokers. You can get 'em from classified ads. They'll be for sale in the commercial real estate section. You can put your own classified ad in there that says, "I buy self-storage," and that will be very--you'll get some good responses from that.

So with direct mail, we've got three rules. The three rules of direct mail are: you're only looking to get a 1% response from your letter. Now, a 1% response, that means that you send out 1,000 letters, you're going to get 10 to 12 to respond to you. And of the 10 to 12 that respond to you, 2 or 3 will be serious sellers.

And of the 2 or 3 that are serious sellers, you may get 1 deal a month. But hey, 1 deal a month – some months you might get no deals and some months 2 or 3. But 1 deal a month – that can start putting some serious cash flow into your pocket very quickly. Storage facilities aren't the type of properties that we're going to flip. We'll flip single families. We'll flip multi-families. We'll flip large commercial properties and small ones. Storage facilities we like to hold, and we like to hold them for Cash Flow. So of the 1% response we have 12 facilities that we put into our Cash Flow bank, and before you know it you're sitting in that hammock by that beach.

Lists are really important. What you want to do is you want to buy an 'Owners of Storage Facilities' list, and you can get it from the different list brokers. You can't really get one of these lists from the assessor's office like you can many other lists, but you can buy them. It will typically cost you anywhere from $0.28 to $0.35 a name.

You may go to a title company to get a list. They may segregate them for you. And if you're really smart, you'll go to your title company. This is what a lot of my students are doing because I told them to. Don't go to the marketing department and ask them if you can buy their list. Go to the department where you would actually use their services, you know if you called up and said, "Hey, I need a title search." Go to that department, and say, "Hey, look, I'm going to use you for my title searches rundowns and to run titles. Could you give me the list of all the people that owned storage facilities in the area?" And if you hit the right person at the right time, they'll give you the list for free. So that's good information.

And then number three, the Headline is the most important part of your letter, whether it be a postcard or whether it be a letter itself. The sole purpose of the Headline is to get them to read the body of the letter. And remember, everybody sorts their mail over the trash. So, in doing that, the whole idea is to get onto the countertop, get on the A pile. And we do that by being interesting.

I don't know if you realize this, but you are actually in the marketing business. You are. No matter what business anybody's in, they're in the marketing business. Real estate happens to be your product, but you're in the marketing business. So, I'm constantly studying marketing, and I'm constantly studying real estate investing.

So, this particular letter says, "I'm interested in buying your property. Read on. Dear Property Owner, I'm interested in purchasing your self-storage facility. Are you interested in selling? I'm currently a member of a group of investors..." – now, if you don't own any storage right now, this is the line that you want to use. If you do own some storage, you want to say, "I currently own x amount of units here." So this says, "I'm currently a member of a group of investors who hold a portfolio of properties similar to yours and are looking to add more." Now, if you're a member of a real estate investment group, you are a member of a group of investors, so that's how you can legitimize that line. "I realize that there are a number of reasons why someone may be interested in selling. Everyone has his or her own reason, and my question to you is: Are you ready to sell? And if so, I am ready to buy. I can close quickly or delay the closing and take as long as you'd like. Please contact me at your earliest convenience so we can discuss the sale of your building. Call me now." That call me now is a call to action, and you need at least two call to actions in your letters. That's very important.

So you know you need a Headline. You know you need two Call to Actions. And then, the second most important part of your letter is actually the P.S. because what's going to happen is they're going to open your letter, they're going to look at the headline and they're going to think, "What is this"? They're going to look down to see who sent it. They're going to look down and see your name. They're not going to know your name, but it's statistically proven that they're going to go from your name over to the P.S. and they're going to read that P.S.

So your P.S. should be the second biggest benefit that they'll get for reading the letter, and it should have a Call to

Action in there. So it says, "To get the best price for your property", because that's the biggest benefit, "call me now at..." The marketing advice that I just gave you works not only with storage, but it also works with any other type of letters that you're sending out for any of your other types of real estate business as well. These ones just happen to specifically work for storage facilities.

So, this particular letter – when you're marketing, there's this phrase called 'Message to Market'. You always are trying to create a good Message to Market. This message to the storage market creates an 8% response on this one letter. So, what you need to do is use the letter over and over and over again. It's a good thing.

Let's talk about Real Estate brokers. Tell them who you are, tell them what you do, tell them what you're looking for, and the most important part of this is to find commonality. And when I say commonality, you want to find something that you have in common with this person. You know you have real estate in common with them, but find something outside of real estate.

Find something – maybe you like to fish, maybe you both like to bake, maybe you like fast cars. Whatever it is, probe a little, probe a little, probe a little until you find something because this is a business relationship, and that's really important to know.

This is a business relationship and relationships are built with people that you have something in common with. People won't do business with you unless they like you and trust you, and they start to like you when you're like them. That's where the commonality comes in, and this commonality is going to give you the opportunity to call your broker once every ten days – that's really important. It's going to give you the opportunity to call that broker once every ten days and feed them some information that may be outside of real estate, but it's something that they're interested in getting. Now, every time you call you're an invited guest instead of a pest.

You're also building up chips, chips in what's called the law of reciprocity. Let's face it, when somebody gives us something we want to give them something in return. If you're constantly giving you're eventually going to get a listing from the broker, and once you do that first deal and perform on that first deal you are off and running because the hurdle is getting over the first one. But when trained properly, you'll get over the first one quickly.

A friend of mine, Steve Hall from Little Rock, Arkansas, bought a 167-unit. The purchase price was $265,000. The value of the property when he bought was $600,000. He's going to be able to refinance it and pull cash out. Now, why was there so much value in the property? Because he found a motivated seller by networking with his real estate broker, and that's what we're looking for as well. We're looking to deal with motivated sellers. As a matter of fact – oh, this was his Acquisition Fee he got for $51,504 at the closing. He automated it with a gate and kiosks and basically has it running by itself. So that was his first deal. Not bad for a first deal. $51,000 in your pocket and $300,000, which he's refinancing right now. He's going to pull out another $300,000. Folks, this is done all the time in this particular business, and that doesn't include the steady increase of the Cash Flow.

We discussed earlier that we get paid three different ways in self storage. We're going to get paid through Cash Flow. The cash flow is the money that we get from our property on a regular basis. We're going to get paid through Appreciation. Appreciation is the money that we're going to get from raising our rents. And then, number three, and my favorite way, is what's called Acquisition Fees.

Our cash flow will include the tenant's rents, "late charges", admin fees and bounced check fees. We will also get paid by creating 'The Store Within Your Facility'. "Ancillary Services Increase your NOI by 20 %.

If you do it right, you're going to have a bunch of different ancillary services, a bunch of different cash flows coming in. Now, here are some of the cash flows that you want to do.

Truck rentals. You can get Rider or you can get any one of those truck rentals companies, you can be a go-to center for them. You don't have to buy their trucks. You just lease their trucks for them and you make a commission off of each truck that gets leased. Easy way to make money because, hey, people need trucks to go to your facility, don't they? So, they rent a truck, they pick up their stuff and they bring it back and they unload, and then the truck is already there. It's a good thing.

Propane fill up is big. You want to have a propane filling station, not only because you'll make money but when people come to your facility for the propane they'll look and they'll say, "Oh, yeah, I might have some stuff that I want to put in there." So it'll actually help you increase your occupancy.

Then there are the boxes. Now, that's a given. Everybody's going to need boxes, so always have boxes on your site and all the different stuff that goes with boxes like tape and those peanut things that go in there that stop things from breaking, and the bubble wrap; all that stuff. And you charge for it all and you make money from it.

eBay centers are big. eBay centers are, you know – there's so many people making a ton of money on eBay right now. But eBay centers here at these particular facilities are moneymakers, as well, because you provide a computer terminal so they can be in there and they can be doing their business. You also provide all the different things that the eBay people need for packing up their goods and sending them out. It's like an office away from home where most people realize that they can't have an office in their home because they don't get anything done.

Business centers themselves – fax machines, copier machines, all the different things that somebody might need to get something done or send something somewhere, or just to get onto the internet for a little while. You can make money on those as well.

Mailboxes. Did you know that you can have mailboxes at your facility? You can actually put an application to the post office and have a mailbox center at your facility. Think about that. With the mailboxes, you'll also have FedEx or UPS. So this will be the go-to place for people to send packages or get their mail. Well, if they're coming to your facility on a regular basis, eventually they're going to think, "Hmm, I could use one of those spaces." Or if they're in a conversation where somebody says they need to store something, they'll say, "Hey, your facility is the place to do it. So this **increases foot traffic**, which will increase your occupancy.

Wine storage is big nowadays. Have special air-conditioned units, very small ones for wine, and get premium prices.

Document storage for businesses is really big as well. You know, most businesses have to keep their documents for seven to ten years.

So that's the hidden Cash Flow in your storage facilities. Not only do you get your rent, but you get all of these extra bonuses if you go out and use them, if you're savvy enough to use them. And in the system, we show you exactly how to step these up and how to profit from them immediately upon buying your facility.

The Rules of Thumb for expenses are based on the Effective Gross Income. These rules apply for a stabilized facility with the occupancy in the 90% range. The Expense to Income ratio will be 30-35% depending on the market. The Total Expense per Rentable Square Foot should be a value in the 3.2 to 3.7 range.

Use the Rules of Thumb when you are analyzing your DEAL.

Taxes = 9 % but Look at the Assessment Value, Verify the taxes, (80% Purchase Price) x (Mill rate) = Taxes Get Mill rate from the assessor's office

Insurance = 2% (this could be higher, depending on if the property is closer to coast, the claim history, if in a flood zone, etc.) A few ways to get cost down: Umbrella policy – when you own a lot of property OR Management Company – if using a management company that manages many properties, you can piggyback on their rate.

Repairs & Maintenance (R&M) = 1% If higher than this - usually from deferred maintenance. Includes Contractors and material

General Administration = 1.5% Misc. things that you need to keep the leasing office running, Accounting Services, Bank Fees, Permits, Office Supplies, Postal Delivery, Telephone, Answering Service, Pagers, etc.

Management Fees Typically 6% of Total Income If you know you are going to be using a particular property manager and you know their fees, use that figure.

Marketing/Advertising = 3.5% If the property is located on a main road or in a tight market they will come in around 2.5%

Utilities = 2% Take historical from last year, annualize this year's, compare & then take the higher of the two. Electricity, Gas, Oil, Water, Sewage

Contract Services = 4% This could be Landscapers, Pest Services, Trash Services, and Security, etc.

Payroll = 3% It is reflective of the area. This is where your lenders become very useful

The Four Keys to a Good Deal
* Low Occupancy
* Room for Expansion
* Additional Income Sources
* Expenses Higher than 35%
Exit Strategies
Wholesale Reposition for Retail

Buy Low Sell High
Hold for Cash Flow

SELF STORAGE REPOSITIONING

The Smell of Money, there is a lot of money to be made in repositioning. It is risky and I would not recommend it if it was your first self storage facility. You want to be cash flowing right out the gate. I am going to show you how to look at this opportunity.

Approach the facility as if you are a tenant who is using storage for the first time and as a tenant who is fed up with your existing storage facility. As you drive to the facility take some notes on the curb appeal or lack of it. What are your first impressions? Does the sign catch your eye? Does it have perimeter fencing and a gate? The exterior is very important. Potential tenants may not even pull into the facility. Ask yourself if you would store your valuable stuff here. Are there any landscape issues? How is the condition of the driveway, walkways and bollards? Do you see a few potholes and cracks?

The Smell of Money. Are the buildings in good shape? Faded and peeling paint on the doors and exterior walls are a big turn off; likewise with the bollards and curbs. Are the storage grounds clean or is there trash and garbage everyway? Do you feel secure as you pull in? Do you see cameras or outside lighting? What, no security system?--another value play. Are there rats running around? Any hornets or yellow jackets flying around? A potential renter thinks about the bad pest problem at his current site. You look at the buildings and there is no systematic numbering on them, you feel confused and think that you will never be able to find your unit,

Low Occupancy 65-75 % The value play here is increasing your occupancy. What is the current occupancy within your 5 mile radius? Determine the market rents in the area. You will be looking for a monthly lease up rate of 2-3.5 % and an annual rental rate increase of 3-5 %

Priority Management

Do they keep the office, the bathrooms and retail area clean? When you walk in is the counter top facing you so you can just walk up to it? Is the carpet worn and not vacuumed?-- nice we like that. Did the retail display end cap catch your eye and make you want to buy a product, or is it dusty, half filled with items that half of them have been opened. Write down in your notes to remove all the duct tape and brown cardboard signs. No retail office?--the smell of money. Is the office well lit?

You will want to visit your competitor to check out their retail centers to get ideas on the changes that you want to make. Use the same vendor for all of your display racks. This will make everything look uniform and consistent. Consult with your retail vendor to get new ideas. The racks should be completely filled with product. The end caps will be your biggest producers. People coming into the leasing office will look at the end caps and buy on impulse.

Painting the leasing office should be done in colors that are warm and bright. Install new bright lights and have as much natural lighting as possible. The leasing counter top should be new or re-laminated and angled and facing the entrance door so that the property manager can greet people. At all times the counter should be free of food, drinks and any other type of debris. The rugs should be fairly new. If your carpet needs to be replaced get a quote on ceramic tile, in some areas it is cheaper than carpet. Ceramic tile is more durable, lasts longer and is easier to clean.

Bathrooms should be clean and well stocked with hand soap and paper products. They should be checked 3 to 4 times a day. All windows and screens should be cleaned on a regular schedule.

The curb appeal of your property can add instant profits. A great looking facility will generate more phone calls and visits from potential renters. A clean facility will project an image of an owner who cares about their business. A renter will feel more at ease storing their valuable items. Create a daily checklist and make sure your contractors clean up afterwards. Find a contractor that will work after non-peak hours in your retail area.

Put yourself in the eyes of the potential renter. Examine the way your facility looks from different areas that surround the facility. Sit in your car at the intersection. Drive past your facility at the posted speed limit. Walk from the parking to the office and around the yard. The facility does not look the same from different angles so you want to make sure you didn't miss anything.

Make sure your **bollards** are looking 'new paint' clean. The bollards may be freshly painted or they may be covered. Bollard covers are a durable poly sleeve, 1/8" thick and they easily slide over the existing bollards (no hardware is needed). They go for about $30 each, are weather resistant, cut down on maintenance and look great. There should be steel bollards at all building corners, entrance gates and entrance/exit key pads. I recommend an 8" steel bollard filled with concrete. Over the years this will save big bucks and a lot of aggravation.

Gravel and dirt driveways should be paved. If you're taking over a facility that has an asphalt driveway, have it resealed and relined. If the existing facility's driveway has a lot of pot holes, you will have to do an overlay. No one likes pot holes. The average thickness for an overlay is 1.5 to 2.5 inches. Once done remember to have a sealant applied every 4 years. This will reduce cracks and extend the life of the driveway. Hint: for concrete stains spread Portland cement over the stain, just enough of the Portland cement to cover it. Let it sit for 24 hours, sweep it up the next day and the stain should be gone.

Have an easy to read sign and make sure that all the lights are working. There are many ways to upgrade your sign. Just make sure that it's cost effective and, most importantly, complies with your city's regulations. A message board with neon lights is becoming very popular with B properties in A areas. Facility owners are posting community event updates, temperature and time. The signs on your buildings should be clear and easy to read, especially the street name and number. If you are going to change your sign you may consider changing the name.

A name change is good, especially if the facility had a bad reputation in the city. Your customer's first impression of your facility is your site sign. Make sure the sign is properly landscaped for a four season sign. Monthly decorations will keep the eyeballs looking in your direction. Pennants (local school colors), flags on the 4th, pumpkins for Halloween, special banners, fall mums, spring bulbs, grasses for the summer and winter are some ideas that should be a part of your site signage.

Keep your landscaping well maintained. Check to see if there is an active landscape contract that you will have to honor until it expires. Review all the details of tasks that have to be performed. Any additional items such as tree trimming may not be on the list.

Get quotes from the existing landscaper and two more. Remove any tree or overgrown shrubs that are a hazard to your buildings, pavement, power lines or that block the view of your facility. All dead shrubs should be removed right away. Add some flower pots and fresh mulch. Check out to see if there is a pest control contract, if so then have them immediately get rid of all insects and rodents.

All Kiosks should have a roof or an awning to protect it and your customers from the rain. The Kiosk itself will be watertight. Since most Kiosks are used 24/7, make sure that it is well lit at night and in a 'feel safe' area. Most Kiosks have warranty plans. Replace any defective part.

The security system may have to be updated. New cameras and monitors may have to be updated or installed. Many facilities are adding individual door alarms. Check the gates and the gate key pad. Existing tenants can be hit with a rent increase to help cover the cost. Determine your competition's security system and make yours equal or better.

Check out the fencing and gates. See if there is still a warranty in effect from the installer, if not and repairs need to be made contact them for a quote. Security is one of the biggest reasons that renters choose one facility over another. Make sure that all the fencing and gates are still intact and have good lines. Add a privacy fence to block out unsightly neighbors. Put the fencing 30 feet off the pavement, if possible, to leave room for snow, especially at the end of long drives.

Make sure that the facility is well lit at night. A lot of renters will only be able to use their units at night. Provide a driveway entrance light at the street. It's been our number one request from tenants.

All unit doors should open and close with ease, tenants get very frustrated if they do not. We will discuss in a moment about what to do about fading colors. The door numbers may have to be replaced since they are also subject to fading and cracking. Replacement door numbers should be easy to read. Vinyl door number will last a long time.

Potential driving by you facility will help you notice the condition of your buildings. Always do the buildings that will be seen first. The buildings should be power washed and then examined after they dry. The power wash will remove the mildew and stains. Be careful around the doors, they are not water tight at the top. The next step would be to treat any buildings or doors that are faded.

Apply a clear coating of EVERBRITE to bring back the original 'like-new' color and add a clear protective covering to stop the fading again. Most of the reasons for fading are from the sun and other weather elements. For peeling paint, I would recommend contacting the manufacturer to get paint specifications and for referrals for painting companies.

The painting contractor must have self storage painting experience. The roll up doors must be repainted with a flexible paint. When you sweep out the unit, sweep any cobwebs and dirt out of the guides on the door.

During your repositioning, your property manager should be sending letters to your renters about the improvements that you are making. These correspondences will be used when you go through the rent raising process.

Do not do a repositioning if you cannot raise rents by at least $5-$20 per unit. Your analysis of the market rents, market occupancy, and your competition would have indicated this, I am just going to repeat it. When you can justify it with your repositioning completions, start with an increase of $10 to your current renters. If you have 200 tenants then you are looking at potentially increasing the cash flow by $2000 per month. If 20 customers decide to move out who are paying an average of $40 per unit then $2000 − (20 tenants) x ($40) = $1200. You stand to make $1200.

If you had only raised the rent by $4 per unit then you would make only $800, and that is if they all stayed. Do you see my point? Plus, with your research you know that the $50 per unit is still at market or a little below. Your property manager is going to notify the tenants and tell them that it is a $10 dollar increase, not that they are now paying $50 per month. This is very important. Most tenants forget what they are paying per month, to them $10 per month increase sounds a whole lot better than $50 per month. Always remember, if they move out then you will have those units for other renters at a higher price. For customers that have 4 or more units you may consider a $7 per unit increase to keep them there.

If you do not want to be so aggressive then do the rate increases at a level that you feel comfortable with. You could do 50 tenants every quarter. If you see significant move outs then stop and re-evaluate how much you should be increasing the rents to your existing tenants and how many new tenants at the higher rate you are leasing up. Implement a solid referral program for your existing tenants. Make them part of the repositioning process.

All of these items should have been picked up during site visit and on your Physical Due Diligence checklist prior to purchasing. The Repair and Allowance clause in your Letter of Intent/Purchase and Sale will provide the funds to make these upgrades. These improvements will retain your current renters and bring in more renters. Keep your facility clean and secure.

A clean, safe facility will be your first phase. You will base your additional upgrades on your location and competition. Ask yourself, "What do I need to upgrade that will allow me to quickly raise my existing rents, attract potential renters and to compete with my competitors?" Repositioning is all about increasing your rental rate and occupancy at the same time while generating retail sales. Reposition so that you can get the rents coming in, so that you can stabilize the property and fund the next phase or your next deal.

Set a goal so that you will be able to personally experience how to **make boatloads of cash with the multiple profit centers available in self storage** including: climate controlled units, tenant insurance, offices, merchandise sales, truck rentals, boat/RV parking and much, much more!

Through everything I have encountered in my investing career, I have discovered that there are basically six keys to creating wealth in real estate. It is these six steps to wealth that you should focus on:

- Finding Good Self Storage Deals
- Quickly and Effortlessly Evaluating the Opportunities

- Negotiating and Writing Offers That Get Accepted
- Raising Capital and $0 Down Commercial Strategies
- Performing Thorough Due Diligence
- Managing to Maximize Income

Create a powerful pipeline that keeps an unlimited amount of deals flowing in endlessly and effortlessly. Steel, Concrete, & Cash Flow. That's a sweet thing. You know what I like best about it, very little maintenance.

In Closing, when it has been said that experience is the best teacher I've come to realize that it's crazy to reinvent the wheel. Instead, I learn from those who have been successful before me—doing the same things that I want to do—I become more successful **much faster**. Aside from reading as many books and listening to as many audios that I can on real estate investing, I also have attended lots of conferences and boot camps. My goal, when I go to these events, is to seek out people that are also successful and see what information I can learn from them to increase my own success.

When talking to these individuals, there is one question that I always ask and am most interested in. That question is **"What was the biggest mistake you made when you first started and, looking back, what could you have done to avoid it?"**

This question usually evokes an odd smile, as these now-successful investors look back into their once-shaky past, and conjure up their biggest folly. Often they will not mention just one situation, but two or three.

The biggest-single quality that each of these investors possess is that when they were struck by adversity, **they did**

not fold up their tents and decide that real estate investing was not for them. They stuck it out and turned each one of their mistakes into a valuable lesson not to be repeated.

The Japanese have a saying: "Fall down 6 times, get up 7." With almost every situation in life—whether it be business, family, relationships, or money—if you adopt this attitude, **you will become unstoppable**.

I created a special report for you called "The 28 Most Costly Mistakes Self Storage Investors Make, And How To Avoid Them" available at www.jeffsfreereport.com

These 28 mistakes come from a blend of my own experiences and the most common responses I've received when I've asked other successful investors to talk about their past.

Go to www.jeffsfreereport.com Download it right now. Read them, study them and don't ever forget them.

To Your Success!
Jeff

How to go from $100 to Millionaire

David Flores

First of all I want to acknowledge you for picking up this book and reading it this far. I know you did it because you feel you are a person who can accomplish greater things in life. Perhaps you felt you've been playing a small game your whole life and you are ready to show the world the real you, the leader you are capable of pursuing and reaching your purpose in life for your own reason. My promise to you is that I'll do my best to inspire you and give you ideas on how to improve your life, and as a consequence, the lives of people around you.

The only request I have from you is that you read this entire chapter and share it with anyone you care about so they can also benefit from my life experiences and principles of success.

Most of my ideas in this chapter are a collection of success principles, universal laws and thoughts taught to me by my mentors, books, audiobooks, home study courses and seminars. I am still a work in progress, and I think I will still be for the rest of my life because I will never know and experience all. There is just not enough time in a lifetime to know it all.

I can honestly tell you that the more I learn the more I find out that I know very little. Anything I mention here is likely an experience, mistake or success I've lived, and I hope you can learn from it and use it to avoid the same mistakes and speed up your path to success. Most of what I wrote here is wisdom that has existed for thousands of years. All I am is one more example that if you follow some of these success principles you can benefit from them. At the end of this chapter I will provide a list of names of all my mentors and sources from which I educated myself, and which you can use too, or you can contact me for an updated list.

Who am I?

I am a lovable, committed father, husband, friend and leader. My name is David Aguilar Flores. I was born and raised in Mexico. I grew up in a magic town called Yanga which is located in the state of Veracruz. Yanga's history claims that it was the first town free from slavery in the American continent.

I emigrated to the U.S. when I was 19 years old with $100 in my pocket. I spoke no English and had no college education, but by the age of 34 years old I was a self-made millionaire through real estate with cash flow rental income above $12,000 every month.

To some $12,000 may not be much but to most it is. This book it's being published in middle of the year 2015 and according to the U.S Census Bureau the average national median household income was $4,328.25 per month as of September 2013.

I own multiple residential single family houses and apartment's buildings in the U.S. and some other single family and commercial spaces in Mexico. Also I am part owner in a 194-unit apartment building controlled by my mentor Dave Lindahl. I am also a real estate broker, and have been one of the top real estate agents in the California Silicon Valley where I have sold over 100 million dollars in real estate to investors-- some of them with real estate purchases that have doubled in value after only 3 to 4 years later.

Investing in real estate does not have to be a gamble. By knowing, identifying and understanding the real estate market cycles you can explode your wealth much faster than most investors out there.

"A tiny change today brings a dramatically different tomorrow" – Richard Bach

My purpose in writing this chapter is to show you that if a 19 year old emigrant with only $100 in his pocket, who spoke no English, can become a self-made millionaire and acquire above $12,000 cash flow from rental income every single month in only a few years, you can too.

Why not you?

By the end of this chapter you will have an idea on how to accomplish it as well, if you choose to. I want to contribute something positive to your life that will inspire you to acquire wealth through real estate. If you just remember one positive thing, concept or meaning I said here, my mission will be done. If it changes at least one degree of your thinking, which I trust it will, it may compound to a big shift of direction after a few years.

I believe that anybody regardless of his nationality, age, sex, background or level of knowledge can also create a life of freedom and abundance if he or she chooses to. The feeling of not having the need to work is one the greatest I have ever experienced, knowing that my bank account will be refilled every single month with rents paid by my tenants. Having the choice to work or not, in my opinion, is the ultimate freedom because it allows you to do what you want, when you want and with whom you want. Working because you love work is the secret to not ever working again.

"Whoever thinks money doesn't buy happiness obviously doesn't know where to shop" - Unknown

---

Cash flow has enabled me to have a comfortable lifestyle. Cash flow is a great friend. It paid for the one year off I took from my business in 2014 and the one month vacations I had in Europe. It pays for my living expenses every month, my utility bills, my nice car and more importantly it helps me to support my son and wife. The cash flow I get from properties I own in Mexico pay for part of my mother's living expenses. It allows me to donate money to charities and help some family members.

Have you heard anybody say that money does not grow on trees? Well, I feel I have a tree of money that I can go to and cut its fruit every month, and it gives me new fruit every month again. My rental income gives me that feeling. I am not saying this to brag about it, my purpose is to inspire you to want the same or more than what I have accomplished.

Do not get me wrong, I am not all about money. I am about what money can do for you, which is give you freedom. Money is a good servant but a bad master. In my opinion, money, if well used, is a vehicle to have more choices in your life so that you do not have to work for money, you have money working for you so you do not HAVE TO!

It gives you the ability to choose your life, and like all things in life you have the choice to see it the way you prefer.

I make money so I can enjoy it with family and friends.

I believe being wealthy or poor is just a state of mind. We can choose to feel wealthy with little and feel poor with a lot. It's our own perspective, and I know because I have experienced both ends. I can tell you that life is much easier when you have money than when you don't have it. I heard somebody say one time, "The best thing you can do for the poor is not being one of them".

I come from a poor family and as a child I knew what it was to have needs. I worked since I was 12 years old so I could support myself to attend school. I am not embarrassed to say we were poor because I overcame it, and even if I were to lose all I have I am confident I can rebuild it because I created skills that will enable me to achieve it again.

One of my mentors, Jim Rohn, said "Pity the man who inherits a million dollars and who isn't a millionaire. Here's what would be pitiful: If your income grew and you didn't." I confidently assure you that anybody who has built something worthwhile has built skills and knowledge that enable them to take action to achieve what they've done.

All what seemed to be terrible life experiences are now my biggest assets. My childhood experiences enabled me to get hungry for success and achievement, especially in the financial area, and again I emphasize this because it's very important if you want to live a life on your terms. Money is a terrible boss (if you only work for it) but it's a great employee (if you have it working for you).

I hope you can convert your terrible life experiences to your most valuable assets. We've all had bad experiences in life, some more terrible than others, but whatever your degree is choose your story. Use your life story as fuel to achieve your goals.

I know people who have said before, and keep saying after a lifetime, that some people were born with good luck and some others with bad luck. All I can tell you about it is that the harder I work, build my skills and improve myself the luckier I get.

"Learn to work harder on yourself than you do on your job. If you work hard on your job you can make a living, but if you work hard on yourself you'll make a fortune." Jim Rohn

Having a positive conversation with Gabriela (my wife) the other day I said, "When we work more than what we are paid for life give us more than what we need. The problem is that most people want to work less that what they are paid for. That is the reason why life gives them less that what they need." Thankfully, I was able to discover this at an early age.

In my opinion, "to be able to have more than what we need, we need to do more than what we get paid in exchange."

That is not something complicated. If what you offer in exchange for payment is a product or a service, your service has to be more valuable to the client than what the client pays for it.

If you are selling a product, your product has to be more valuable to the client than what the client paid. Let me give you an example; I am a real estate broker and 100% of the time I get my clients more money and/or less problems for their real estate than the cost of my commission (compared to selling their real estate themselves).

The first job I got was as a dishwasher making $5.25 per hour at a bakery and cafe in Sunnyvale, California. I worked there for about three months until I asked a coworker how much the manager was making per hour. The answer was $10 dollars per hour, then I knew that if I aspired to get to a higher financial level and to be the café manager I was not going to get very far with $10 per hour. Shortly after that I discovered that bakers in the same company were making $20 dollars per hour.

I asked that manager to transfer me to a bakery section so I could be a baker. I never thought in my life that I would be a baker. How many people in their lives end up on a job they never planned to work on? Did something similar happen to you?

Did you know when you were a child what job you would like to do when you were an adult? Have you discovered your passion on a job yet? Just something to think about.

Then, three years later I was a baker making $21 per hour. I was accepted into the union so I had all union benefits: retirement, medical plan and paid vacations. I worked there for a total of seven years and my plans were to work there for another thirty-three years so I could retire with a baker's union pension and a social security pension. The average retired baker at the time I worked there was making about $4,000 from those two pensions combined after working forty years of his/her life as a baker.

I never imagined that seven years later, after I left that job at that bakery, I would be making over $12,000 a month cash flow from my real estate investments. That's three times the amount a baker got as pension and social security after working forty years of their life. Can you imagine what I could have lost if I stayed there? And the most important question is, what could you lose in your life if you do not work to achieve your dreams?

Life looked good for me at that time. I had an average job with an average life, but deep down inside my heart I was not happy. I felt I did not belong to that job! I never felt complete. I am not talking about the money. I now know I was not happy at that job because I was not doing what I felt passionate about, I was not exploiting my higher potential.

If you enjoy what you do as a job or business, congratulations! You are one of the very few who do, if not you need to consider it and get clear about what is it that you really want in life and just go for it. Life is too short to wake up one day and discover that it is the last day of your life and you never did what you enjoyed doing?

What can you now do so at some point you will be able to live life in your own terms and be happy about it? If you want to get clear I suggest you get a piece a paper and write it down. You will be surprised what will come out.

Suddenly life change comes to our lives, whether we want it or not. At the bakery where I worked our dayshift general manager, who worked there for at least thirty years, was retiring and the night shift general manager was taking over as general manager for both the day and night shifts. The new general manager's purpose was to overlap night and day shifts at the bakery to save money and increase the bakery profits. He started implementing changes so the bakery would save money for the company, such as reducing employee benefits, laying off some employees, and increasing the work load to employees who stayed for the same pay and hours worked. He changed our schedules so some days we would start working at 4am and the next at 8am and the next at 6am to accommodate more of the company's needs and save money to the company.

Then he approached me and asked me if, under his supervision, I wanted to become a foremen of the night shift where I would manage approximately another thirty bakers at any given time. I agreed to become one of the night shift foremen. He started to fix my work schedule in a way that one day I would work day shift, take one day off, and then work night shift just so the company can save over time on other employees.

> *"It's in the moments of decision where your destiny is shaped. Tony Robbins*

My natural inclination at that time was to blame him for the unwanted changes that made me uncomfortable in my life. How could he come in and change the work to overnights in a way that affected me negatively. It all pointed to me that he wanted to show the company owners they had made the right decision in making him the new general manager by showing the owners how much money he would save the company (at employees' expense), but in reality it was just a life's wake up call for me.

We all get those in life sooner or later if we like it or not, and in one of those moments decisions are made that shape our lives. I decided to quit that job at the bakery and start on my own at real estate. It was what I have always wanted to do ever since I was a child, but it was not easy to leave what I believe was a "secure job with secure pay". It was scary. I remember after I left that job, I would wake up in the middle of the night and ask myself "what if I do not do well as a real estate agent? What if I have to go back to the bakery?"

One day I decided to just go for it and put all I had toward the success of my new career, and I am so glad I did! This time I made sure I did what I wanted to do. I always liked people and I wanted to use real estate as a vehicle to acquire rental properties and live off of the rents, just like the two wealthiest people in my small home town, Doña Carmen and Don Aquiles (Miss Carmen and Mr. Aquiles). Those persons owned lots of real estate in my home town, and their stories were similar to each other.

I heard that both came to Yanga, Veracruz (my home town) from another city. They arrived with nothing, and after many years they were the wealthiest people in town and owned houses here and there and there. I remember one day I started counting the houses they owned and adding the rents they were collecting every month, and to my surprise it was more than any average blue collar worker would make in a whole year. That day I decided I wanted to be like them because they were so respected.

The day before I left the bakery I was told by another foremen that the new general manager had a heart attack the night before and he was taken to the hospital. Nobody knew when he would be back to work again. I was asked by the company owners if I wanted to delay my time to leave the company for another two weeks. I declined the offer. I said I had already decided to leave and it was all planned.

I left and continued to work on my real estate business right away. I stayed in touch with a couple of coworkers from the bakery and a few months later they told me the new general manager recovered his health and was back in the bakery continuing with the changes to save more money for the company. Things were getting worse for them. They seemed to not be happy at all with all the new changes this guy was making.

Approximately six years after I left the bakery one of those former coworkers told me the new general manager (not so new now) was called into the office of the company owners and he was told that they were downgrading his position from general manager to just a baker. They would decrease his salary as well because they were hiring a new person to take over for him as general manager, and that new person taking over for him had a higher level of education and training than he did on how to run the bakery as general manager. A couple of days after he was informed about his downgrade from general manager to a simple baker he left the bakery, wow!

Here is a universal law, 'What Goes Around Comes Around'. Universal laws, you may have never heard of them but that does not exclude you from their effects, these are laws like gravity and Karma and are not enforced by mankind but they are enforced by whatever you choose to believe in: God, universe or nature.

I did not even know such laws exist, but not knowing that they exist does not mean it does not work for you or against you as all in life have both sides, the positive or the negative. I never had the opportunity to thank my former boss for shaking my world and forcing me to make a decision that now put me in a better life position.

I still hear from one of the guys at the bakery that things have gotten worse, their baker pensions seemed to not have been funded anymore, the medical coverage has been reduced in half and people are not getting as much social security retirement payments as before.

I like to know what keeps happening with the employees at that bakery because it reaffirms that I made the right decision, as it all seems it keeps getting worse and worse for them.

So this part of my life about leaving the bakery is one of those moments that we all experience in life when we feel life or someone is unfair to us, and that something should have not happened. But only after many years you wake up one day and realize that it was one of the greatest things that had happened in your life.

I now understand what God or the universe planned for me. At that moment I did not understand. I was only focusing the blame onto the new general manager in my mind. It's very hard to predict ahead of time what a life changing event will become years later, and only the future knows if this chapter will have a positive impact on your life years later.

One example of this could be the classic movie "Matilda". Roald Dahl's work tells the story of Matilda, a gifted little girl forced to discover and develop her talents due to her parent's indifference and her bully teacher Trunchbull. If you have not seen it, it's a fun movie.

Another defining moment in my life was while working at the bakery. I owe this life changing moment to Jose Toscano who was a coworker at the bakery. One day he approached me approximately four years after I started working at the bakery and told me, "David I have a gift for you that I believe you'll like." It's a set of CDs I will let you borrow from me". He was introducing me to a Robert Kiyosaki audio book "Rich Dad Poor Dad." That audio book totally changed my mindset and thinking about money.

That's the first time in my life I had heard the term that money can work for you so you do not have to. You never know what a book, somebody's words or actions can do in someone's life.

At that moment I knew I wanted to accomplish the same financial freedom Robert achieved and explained in his book. And guess what, years later I discovered I did it. I wanted to own rental properties just like Robert explained in his book, and just like the properties Dona Carmen and Don Aquiles owned in my home town. I was inspired to discover that someone had a formula for doing what I wanted to achieve as my life project.

I was inspired to know that someone had a road map to achieve what I wanted and was sharing it.

I asked myself what it would feel like to achieve what Robert Kiyosaki did, which was receiving rental income and being financially free. That revelation led me to the real secret of wealth. It's that a good investment, not a job, can free your life sooner than a job can do by retirement pension or social security.

"The poor and the middle class work for money.
The rich have money work for them."
Robert Kiyosaki

By reading "Rich Dad Poor Dad" I ignited something powerful called awareness. I discovered a new perspective about life, a new way to see things, and that is the first step to creating progress.

Have you ever wanted something so badly and you have no idea how to get it? Well, I believe that that's where the law of attraction begins. When you want something, and you have a burning desire to get it, the universe will conspire so you get it.

So, for me the first step was discovering what I did not know that I did not know-- that money can work for me so I do not have to. What a great concept. It felt like creating a slave out of money that would work for me and bring me even more money, and if invested wisely it will get stronger and duplicate itself and will double, triple and quadruple itself.

Once I discovered what I did not know about money I then was able to do something about it, therefore, the importance of reading books like this, listening to audio books or attending seminars so you can become aware of what you do not know that you do not know.

Seeing life from somebody else's perspective ignites new possibilities, new ways to do things. It expands our world, and accomplishments once impossible can become possible.

So, I started my journey looking to learn what I did not know, and shortly after I discovered that the only difference between the people who had the type of life I wanted to build and I was the way they think. All human beings have the same capacities to expand and learn, and one commonality on each of the successful people I know that have the life I wanted was they keep always educating themselves. They keep learning and expanding their potentials.

At that moment I discerned that the only way I could become financially free was by educating myself, by acquiring as much knowledge as quickly as possible. I decided to use real estate as a vehicle to achieve this financial freedom, so I decided to become a real estate agent. I thought to myself, "what better way to learn all about buying, selling and renting real estate than by doing it."

Becoming a real estate agent is not necessarily the only way to create wealth in real estate, but that's what I chose and it worked for me. I found that it is something I love to do and I am passionate about it. I enjoy being involved in buying and selling of real estate, and that makes me more effective doing it. People always tell me, "we like your energy when you speak about real estate," and I always say, "it's because it's not a job for me it's something I love to do."

If you want to change your life, change your thinking. There is no faster and more efficient way to change your life than to change your thinking. Just think about it, every time you or somebody changes their life it starts with a thought or decision for a new way to do things. In order to do things differently you need to change your thinking. Where you are is a result of your current thinking, and if you keep doing more of the same you will continue getting the same of what you already have. If you really want to change your thinking and go to new places and experience new results, your new thinking has to be strategic. It has to be something that will increase your knowledge or awareness in the area you want to improve.

Once you change your inside world or thinking your outside word or results automatically change.

"The single most powerful asset we all have is our mind. If it is trained well, it can create enormous wealth in what seems to be an instant."

— *Robert T. Kiyosaki, Rich Dad, Poor Dad*

The first thing I did was I went to look for mentors and teachers, people who could teach me how to achieve my goals faster. As Jim Rohn said, "Let me ask you something. If you want to improve your health, which book are you reading about health? If you want to improve your business, what business book are you reading? If you want to be a great parent, what parenting book are you reading? If you want to be rich, what wealth books are you reading?"

So any area that needs to be mastered needs to be studied. There are books, seminars, classes, instructional DVDs to teach us each one of those areas, and coaches to keep us accountable for results. Still it is up to us to become masters by doing the work required to become a master at that subject.

I discovered that in order to change I needed to change my mindset, forcing myself to do things worked but just temporarily. In order to create lasting change we have to change the way we think. Oprah Winfrey once said in an interview, "I always wanted to help people and one time I failed miserably." Oprah said she went and built houses on a country outside of the United States and gave them to poor people so they could have a better life. Shortly after she found out that most of those persons sold or lost the houses she gave them. She said the reason was because she changed their world from the outside but their mindset was still the same.

Right at that moment I discovered that if I wanted to help myself or anybody else I needed to change my way to think. If Oprah had changed the mindset of those poor people they could have built houses for themselves and kept them, and as a consequence improved the quality of their lives.

The way I applied that on my life is when I wanted to lose weight. I had to change my mindset about being overweight and understand the way it negatively affected my life. In order to achieve it, I needed to alter my reality. In order to alter my reality, I needed to get new information to replace what I already have in my brain. Our brains are like computers, we need to upgrade to a newer software to stay efficient. Just like the computer upgrades its software every certain time, we need to do the same to our brain if we want to grow and improve.

Here are just some of the ways that worked for me.

(1). Getting ourselves around people who've been there and done that. Look for people who were overweight and lost weight and kept the weight permanently off. Look for at least three people like that; interview them, ask them questions understand what their turning point was, what method or technique helped them lose weight. Ask what were the mistakes they did on their journey to lose weight? (so you can avoid those mistakes). Find commonalities to your situation. Be close to them. Bring benefits to their life so they are happy to welcome you to their life, and you will see how you will start picking up some of their habits.

We have a human need to feel connected or related to the persons that surround us. If everyone around us were fit and healthy it would become the normal in our lives, and if we were the only ones unfit or unhealthy we would feel unconnected or unrelated to everyone in our circle.

Proximity is very important, and like most things it works both ways positively and negatively. On the negative side, if we are the only fit and healthy ones in our circle and everyone around us were unfit and unhealthy it's very likely everyone around us will want to drag us to be unhealthy like them.

My mother use to say, "tell me who your friends are and I will tell you who you are."

(2). Read books about the topic you want to improve on. Read at least three bestsellers books on the topic of losing weight. I guaranteed you it will change your way of thinking about health. To me reading a book is like absorbing someone's wisdom, experiences and expertise about a particular topic. It's like having the book's author giving me a private class with all of his or her attention just for me. I was able to lose forty pounds by following this method. Reading books in my opinion, is the easiest, fastest and most inexpensive way to alter our reality.

The reason why things you wanted to improve before did not last long enough to become a habit is because you changed the way of doing things by forcing yourself, but did not change your mindset. Changing your mindset makes progress inevitable and effortless. It's something you cannot avoid. Change is eminent whether we want it or not. "Man's mind, once stretched by a new idea, never regains its original dimensions," said by Oliver Wendell Holmes

(3). Take action! This is the one where most of us fall short, as taking action is where the rubber meets the road. It is where magic really starts happening, a concept that really hit me hard on the book I read, "6 months to 6 figures." Peter Voogd said something like this, "I'd rather read three books a year and master them than read fifty books and not master them." So what has worked for me is to get a coach for the area I want to improve. Knowing all things we need to do to achieve what we want is not enough, we need accountability, knowing that someone will be asking you what did you eat yesterday makes you think twice before you put that piece of cake in your mouth. That's how I personally feel when I know my CrossFit coach, Ronny Varghese, will ask me, "What did you eat yesterday? What are you eating today? And what will you eat tomorrow?"

A coach has to be someone who is an expert in the area you want to improve and has to have achieved something bigger than what you want to achieve because only that way he or she will be able to guide you and coach you to faster, bigger and better results than you can imagine.

A coach will be able to identify the areas you are weak in and guide you to focus on improving the most needed skills to achieve your goals. If you do not know the correct way to do something you may become experts at doing the wrong thing and get discouraged for not getting results.

For example, my CrossFit coach, Ronny, has been working on my posture. When doing weight lifting they taught me that by having the right posture I could double my results in half of the time. I prevent hurting myself and it helps me to have a better posture even when I am not weightlifting, which gives me a better physical appearance.

Just a slight change like that can give us exponential results. Imagine that just doing the correct posture, he is not asking me to add more time to the exercise or double my efforts, just a slight change on the way I do it. Do you see how powerful it is to have a coach in any area you want to succeed? So, get a coach!

> *"Most people fail to realize that in life, it's not how much money you make, it's how much money you keep." — Robert T. Kiyosaki, Rich Dad, Poor Dad*

Continuing with my plan to create wealth, I first started saving money so I could invest it. Although some real estate gurus will tell us we do not need money to invest because we can use other people's money, I still believe I need to be able to learn how to produce and administrate my own money before I go and invest other people's money.

I feel much more confident to administrate or invest other people's money when I can show them that I am capable of multiplying and investing successfully my own money. I once heard someone say that when hiring a financial adviser ask the advisor being hired how financially strong he or she is. His or her answer will tell a lot about how they will handle my money to be invested. Do not get me wrong, I believe investing other people's money creates a win-win situation for both parties, the one investing the money and the investor because both owe it to each other to generate profits out of an investment.

As a word of caution I would suggest that if you are the investor you must really make sure the person you are investing with knows very well the investment strategy, what's the potential profit and the exit strategy, preferably someone with a track record of investment success or in the type of investment being done.

I consider myself a conservative investor. I only invest in investments I know and with people I trust, and I always make sure they really know what they are doing. The person who you are investing with must have your best interest in mind.

At the beginning, while creating my wealth goal, I worked very hard to save money. Once I had a considerable amount, I invested it and re-invested its profits. I always followed one principle, which was to keep my expenses below my means. I never expended more than what I earned and, fortunately, that created a habit that I still practice.

As a rule of thumb you should start saving 10% of all your take home income if you are not already doing it. I was saving at least 35% of all my income and then reinvesting its investment profits. I had another year of savings, and repeated the same formula again for three consecutive years until I started investing in real estate.

I know this formula is not sexy to some and is not the only formula, but I can assure you that for thousands of years many fortunes have been build this way.

"The man who became of his understanding of the laws of wealth, acquireth a growing surplus, should give thought to those future days. He should plan certain investments or provisions that may endure safely for many years, yet will be available when the time arrives which he has so wisely anticipated." The Richest Man In Babylon by George S. Clason

I can confidently assure you that if you follow this formula and are diligent about it over the years your investment income will exceed your full time job income. That could help you create your financial freedom to retire early, or you could have time to increase your skill knowledge to find a new job or career that you enjoy doing (in case you have a job you do not enjoy). I said this because according to a 2013 report by the Conference Board, the New York-based nonprofit research group, 52.3% of U.S. workers are dissatisfied with their jobs. More than half of U.S. workers dislike their jobs.

It means that more than five people out of every ten you see on the street have a job they are not happy to go work every day.

I recommend anyone to find a job that they are passionate about. It will increase his or her level of happiness and potentially more income, because it would not feel like work anymore. It would feel like something you want to wake up and do every single day. Your mind will be more positive and I believe a positive mind brings positive outcomes. I have always believed that the more money you have the easier to make more. That seems to be one of the universal laws, 'Money Attracts Money.'

> *"I learned how to become wealthy because I asked the right questions when I was broke." -*
> *Mark Cuban*

Although I was living within my means, we never felt we missed anything because I always covered all our basic necessities. You will be surprised how many things we buy that we do not need. I have had countless things in my garage that I've purchased that I never used, things that I many times purchased by impulse, not because I needed them but because they was on sale.

Having a wealth plan allowed me to pay attention to my finances and stop buying things I did not need. I made a conscious decision to ask myself, "Do I really need that thing I am about to purchase? Is owning this thing going to make my life easier? Can I use something else I already own instead?"

If the answer to the first two questions is no, and yes to the third question, then I would not buy it. I believe we save much more money by not buying stuff we do not need, than by buying at a discounted price. I laugh every time I see or hear a retail advertisement saying "save money by buying more."

Actually, by owning less stuff your life is simpler and therefore easier. Do you feel it takes mental space when you have a garage or storage full of things you need to get rid of, and you go and clean out and feel better, and then find it full again a few months later? Well then, the solution is to buy only what you need. Do not buy stuff you do not need. Come out with your own set of questions to yourself if you like, or use mine, to find out if you really need it or not.

Believe it or not it is all connected, one thing leads to another. That is another important principle, that success is one of the universal laws, it is the law of connection that says that the universe is connected, each step leads to the next step and so forth and so on. Changing one simple habit such as not buying stuff you do not need would create a new habit of preserving your wealth and peace of mind.

My plan was not to live frugally my whole life, my plan was to have my investments pay for my nice cars and a house bigger than what my family and I needed so I could enjoy life while my investments pay for items I enjoy.

I was careful to not start spending my investment profits on things that would NOT produce for me more earnings, until the profits are enough to cover my basic living expenses.

I am always looking for more real estate investments that will bring me a good return on investment, and I can tell you that at some point if you keep repeating this formula your investment earnings will pay for your living expenses and your luxury life if you choose too.

We just need to be patient at the beginning. We all have material possessions we wish to own. I can assure you that the more money we earn the more expensive are the things we want to possess. Making more money creates a new possibility of owning something we were not able to own before because of its cost.

It may become easy to justify a non-existing need, therefore, it's important to create the habit of not buying what we do not need in order to preserve the new wealth to be created by investing. As I said, I am always looking for real estate deals to invest in. So, if you come across a multifamily apartment building or commercial real estate deal that brings at least a 9.5% cap rate go to my website Davidsbookclub.com and submit the deal information. We could become partners and profit from it. I may fund the deal and bring my investing experience.

You may be thinking, saving money you want me to save money when I just make enough to pay my living expenses? My answer is "yes", unless you give up and accept to keep living the same life you have you have to make changes. You cannot expect to get different results by doing the same things over and over again. You may have heard that's the definition of insanity.

The Law of Cause and Effect is one more of the Universal Laws and it states that "For Every Action There is an Equal and Opposite Reaction." I believe that common sense tells us that if the action is positive the consequence will generally be positive and if negative we generally get negative results.

Here is one more you may have hear; "We reap What We Sow." Again, depending on the action, it can be negative or positive. The choice is yours. You may be thinking, "where do I start?" So here are some ideas. Do not eat at restaurants or fast food places frequently, cook at home and eat at home. It will save you money, it also helps us eat healthier. Do not buy expensive cups of coffee, brew your own coffee at home.

Rather than going to the movies go to a park, spend some time in nature where it will not cost you as much. Remember these are not things you have to do forever, it is only for a few years until your investments pay for your living and recreational expenses, your luxury life, and why not? Do you see how these are changes you can make to save and keep your money.

Once I had a good amount of money saved I started investing in real estate. I started buying when the real estate market was in its worst shape. Everyone was running away from real estate. There were lots of foreclosures happening. I knew it would not last forever and I knew property values would go up sooner or later. I totally believe that every problem represents an opportunity, so when I purchased my first investment house for $210,000 and one year later, after spending about $20,000 on repairs, I sold it for $330,000 making a nice $120,000 profit, then I repeated the process multiple times.

When I saw the real estate market picking up, I started buying rental properties to keep them, and now some of those rental properties have more than doubled in value and the cash flow they produce every month keeps increasing every year as rents increase.

I typically looked for rental properties in areas where property values are low but rents are high. I have seen many investors make the mistake of buying rental properties where property values are high and rents are low.

Let me give you one example of what I mean; one of the rental properties I purchased in Oakland, California cost me

$140,000 and produces me a monthly rental income of $2,300 while the house where I live in San Jose, California cost me $700,000 and the rents for similar houses are going for $3,000 a month. Do you see the difference?

If you'd like to know more about the areas where property values are low and rents high, go to the website I created for this book at www.Davidsbookclub.com and get your free report "The Most Profitable Landlord's U.S Cities", I will be glad to share it with you.

I am constantly watching these areas of the country where rents are low comparably to the property value, but sometimes values go up quickly. The most important thing is to purchase the properties while still low in value and rents are high comparably to property value, or starting to increase.

When investing in real estate it is very important to have some knowledge about real estate market cycles or have someone on your team who knows about it and can identify what cycle is the real estate market you are investing in; whether a Seller's Market Stage One, Seller's Market Stage Two, Buyers Market Stage One or Buyers Market Stage Two.

Buying the right property at the right time makes all the difference on whether you will profit or have a loss, how much profit there can be and what exit strategy will be best. Thanks to my Real Estate Mentor, Dave Lindahl, who taught me how to identify those market cycles, I was able to invest in the right property at the right time so I could ensure a profit. I have always invested conservatively. I believe that by knowing your investments you are not betting but making educated investments.

That is the reason I decided to learn from Dave Lindahl. He has been able to guide me to increase my wealth by teaching me how to invest in apartment buildings. I have been in his coaching program for a short time, and by using his teachings about investing in apartment buildings in emerging markets I am now part owner of a 194 unit apartment building in Florida, which also brings me cash flow and I love it.

My next plan is to keep expanding by investing in apartment buildings and commercial real estate in emerging markets and properties with a value play. Believe it or not there are always emerging markets in the United States at any given time, even during the mortgage meltdown of 2008 there were markets in which properties were going up in value.

Multifamily properties are valued by the income they produce, so if you increase the rents you also have increased the value of the property. It also helps minimize the losses because, unlike single family houses where I have one tenant, if the tenant moves out I am now losing 100% of rental income.

On the other side, if I own an apartment building of 100 units and 10 of the tenants move out I still have 90% of the income that building produces. Also, it is easier to replace one roof of a 100-unit building than 100 roofs on 100 houses. And, when I own a 100-unit apartment building, the investment produces enough income to hire a property manager so I do not have to be managing the property day in and day out myself.

I still own multiple single family houses as rentals and I love the cash flow they produce. For some who do not feel comfortable to start with an apartment building, it is a good way to get started and get familiar with tenants' business until you feel comfortable to start investing on bigger projects. I suggest to anybody to start investing in real estate with as little money as possible, then re-invest its profits to create bigger profits, then invest on bigger investments.

> *"Formal education will make you a living; self-education will make you a fortune."* - Jim Rohn

The next step in my journey to creating wealth was, and still is, to invest in myself. Once I owned multiple rental properties and had good income from those properties my responsibilities to my tenants and properties increased. It was imperative for me, as a real estate investor, to upgrade my knowledge so I could make better decisions based on the ownership of multiple rental properties. Even if I have a property manager managing all my properties I still need to understand what is going on with my properties.

I discovered that the bigger my investments are the easier it is to make bigger mistakes. Therefore, I decided to invest in my real estate education. I started learning about emerging markets and real estate market cycles. I invested quite some time and money attending dozens of real estate and personal development seminars, reading books, listening to audio books and doing home study courses.

Have you ever heard somebody say that they lost their fortune because they did not know something? Well that is the main reason why we need to keep upgrading ourselves and our knowledge, so we have an idea ahead of time what is coming and we can prevent or prepare for it.

It is also very important to have the right attorneys, accountants and real estate brokers on your team so they can advise and help you avoid costly mistakes. On the other side, have you ever heard somebody say they built a fortune because they were at the right place, moment and time? And although those are important factors for a great opportunity I still believe we have to be prepared for when the opportunity shows up.

I am talking about prepared with knowledge. Have you ever identified opportunities to make massive amounts of money after the opportunity was gone, if only we knew that before. Well, it will keep happening. There will always be opportunities to build fortunes, and I discovered that there is always someone who knows about it and will profit from it.

I think our job then is to learn what is next and be ready to act when the opportunity shows up, or to find the persons who know and to learn from them. In my case I found my multifamily apartment investments coach, Dave Lindahl.

Fortunately, one of my greatest passions is learning. I really enjoy learning. I personally believe we do not need to know every single thing but we just need to know all we possibly can in our careers or lines of work so we can serve as many people as possible, and in my case it's real estate investment.

I believe that to build great wealth we need to serve as many people as possible by solving their problems. I always think about what I do to earn money as resolving someone's problem. For example, I am a landlord, real estate agent and investor; as a landlord I am resolving somebody's problem of a need for a place to live. How do I resolve the problem? I rent them out a place to live and in exchange they pay rent.

As a real estate agent, I resolve someone's need to sell their real estate by selling it for the highest amount possible, with the least amount of hassle, and in the shortest time possible. In exchange they pay me a commission.

As an investor I solve someone's problem of selling a house or building that is in disrepair or has a problem that will stop an average buyer from buying it. How do I resolve the problem? I pay cash for the building to the seller, and the seller in exchange sells me the building with a discount so I can fix it and resell for a profit.

In my opinion the real path to wealth is solving as many problems for as many people as possible. Now, we can do an average job or we can do an outstanding job. Personally, I live to do an outstanding job because it brings me repeat business, it creates my reputation and clients bring me more clients.

My mindset the whole time is just to resolve as many problems as possible. Investing and upgrading myself constantly gives me the ability to solve problems more efficiently.

Investing in ourselves includes taking care of our minds and bodies every single day. I can honestly tell you there is not a better investment than investing in our bodies and minds period, none.

Understating this is imperative for anyone wanting to have an extraordinary life. We need to constantly be learning and improving our knowledge in any area of life we believe is important, but I think it is crucially important to learn as much as possible about our psychology and to reinforce our positive thinking. Just think about it for one minute, we were given a brain but we were not given a manual on how to operate it. Our brain is like a super powerful computer and yet some of us do not take the time to learn how to use it effectively.

For example, the idea that thoughts become feelings, feelings become actions, and actions become results. This is fundamental for any type of success we want to achieve in life. So, everything starts with a thought.

It is of extreme importance to learn how to use our brains properly because, believe it or not, we can choose our thoughts. We can choose what to think about, therefore, we can choose our results. Our minds and our bodies are connected, they are totally connected. If either one is not well the other is not well either. If you do not believe what I say go for a run in the morning after a good night's sleep. The run has to be at least 30 minutes long and as intense as you can run. Once you come back from running eat a healthy breakfast, and you will see how you will feel much more relaxed the rest of the day. You will have more energy during the day and you will see how focused and productive you will be on that particular day.

Now imagine if you can repeat the same thing every single day of your life, would you become a relaxed and focused person? So, is there a connection between mind and body? The answer is yes.

We can be the greatest investor in the world and make tons of money, but what sense would it make if our bodies have pain, or we have a short life? I do not know about you but I want to enjoy this ride called life while I can, so when the moment I have to leave comes I can said I did it all as I wanted to do.

Just as I said real estate was a vehicle for me to achieve wealth, my body is my vehicle for everything I am and I want to do. For people like me who are focused on achievement, it is very easy to forget to take care of ourselves, our bodies and our minds.

For me it is harder to rest than to keep working. Thankfully, I have my wife Gabriela who reminds me frequently to enjoy life and take some time off. I have built the habit of working out every single day. I do it mostly in the morning as early as possible. Anybody can do it, it is like anything hard at the beginning but becomes easier later. I have reached a point that I must do it every single day or I would feel like I was missing something.

Building any new habit on average takes 90 days. Some say 21 days but for me to get it engrained to a point I cannot stop doing it is 90 days. I guess it may depend on the habit you are building.

"Success is not something you achieve, it is something you attract by the person you become" Jim Rohn

Let's not forget that in order to accomplish anything we need to have energy, and the ripple effect about health touches energy. Any action we take or do not take creates a reaction good or bad. For example, for some of us if we fail to exercise every day or maintain a healthy diet our levels of energy will go down and our body will start gaining weight.

The problem with this concept is that we do not realize we are unhealthy the same day we eat one hamburger or fail to exercise. It takes years to realize that after we have been forming habits of unhealthy eating. It would be great if we could measure our unhealthiness at the end of each day when we eat a hamburger.

Health, like the mind takes time. Most of us cannot read and learn a book in one day, our brain processes information in small portions for better retention. That is the reason why it's easier to remember smaller phrases than larger ones. It's the same way with our health, it's an everyday job.
We are unable to lose forty pounds in one day, neither can we gain them in one day.

I picked up a concept from Jim Rohn that has changed my life. He said, "Miss a meal if you have to, but don't miss a book." He was talking about building the habit of reading every day.

Now that I have explained how I achieved my financial goal, you see it's not complicated. It takes commitment, time and perseverance. Choose your financial goal. Choice is one of the most powerful possessions each one of us has. You can choose to be rich even if you do not have millions. You can choose to be happy even if you are going on difficult times. You can choose to be a success even if you are not being acknowledged by everyone around you.

It is all in our mind. My childhood was not a comfortable one but that has empowered me to be the person whom I am now. I chose my story and I choose happiness regardless of the circumstances sounding my external world. Some of the circumstances I can control and some others I cannot, but my internal world certainly can be controlled and I am the only one who has the control, positive and negative.

Same for you, whatever is a difficult time you are facing now or you have faced in the past, choose the opportunity to turn it into fuel that will burn in your heart to give you the energy to show the world who you really are and what you are made of.

We can either choose good or bad thoughts. The choice is individual for each one of us, it works both ways all good or bad. At the same time you can choose to feel poor even if you have millions. You can feel unhappy even when you are having the best moment of your life, or feel a failure even when everyone around you wishes to have your success.

Our worst enemy is not the one that conspires against us, our worse enemy is our mind. Is this so basic? If your answer is "yes" my question to you is, have you conquered? Have you mastered your mind? Are you able to transform any adversity into fuel to create the life you are happy to live? If your answer is yes, congratulations! You are extraordinary, you are a minority, a rare breed of people who has discovered the biggest lie of the world, according to Paulo Coelho author of "The Alchemist", where he states in his great book of wisdom that the biggest lie of the world is that at some point in our lives we lose the control of our lives at that moment our lives are controlled by our destiny.

Our beliefs create our own reality. The Chinese philosopher Confucius said, "He who says he can and he who says he can't are both usually right."

"The practice of gratitude can increase happiness levels by around 25%...Gratitude

enriches human life, it elevates, energizes,
inspires and transforms. Gratitude improves
emotional and physical health, and it can
strengthen relationships and communities." –
Robert Emmons

Life is about the journey, not the end result. I keep this adage in a place very near to my heart since for many years for me it's been all the end result. After earning my first million dollars I discovered that I was there. Nothing really extraordinary happened. Nobody cares if you have a million dollars or not unless you are going to share it with them, but then you will not be a millionaire anymore.

Author Bronnie Ware, in her book "The Top Five Regrets Of The Dying," states that the second most common regret people have when dying is that they worked too much and never made time for their family. Once I was financially free, I discovered that I did not want to spend the rest of my days on a beach under the sun. After a few days, or for others after a few weeks, you get tired of it. We all have different natures, mine is about expanding, improving, serving and contributing. So I decided to take one year off in 2014, and what I discovered is that I just got slow and sluggish. It was like oversleeping, it just made me feel worse.

I never felt 100% rested so I came back to work, but this time I decided to enjoy every single thing I do. I decided to work at my business but also at the same time on my body, my well-being and my relationships.

I am totally convinced we do have the power to work in all those areas at the same time and still enjoy life. We can enjoy simple things such as changing a baby's diaper, or having an important negotiation with a difficult client. We can enjoy feeling the pain in our body while working out. It is just a mind shift.

I can choose to enjoy the pain of my body while exercising because it makes me stronger, and I know that I will feel much better once I rest. My energy levels will increase at the same rate of the intensity of the exercise I did. Choose to embrace whatever situation you are going to. Think about it, whatever you are doing you still may have to do it even if you do not like doing it.

So why not start pretending you enjoy it and see what happens. You will have a happier life and get better results. Remember, thoughts create feelings, then actions, then results-- so choose your thoughts to happy ones and your chances for better results will increase. Attitude is important because you still have to deal with whatever happens and it's easier to deal with difficult situations with a good attitude than a bad one.

Whatever you are going to do in life, whether you like it or not, there is a reason. God, or the universe, has a master plan for you, and I like to think everything is put in front of us for a good reason. It is up to us to choose our reason.

I personally can tell you my life struggles are my biggest assets. They have become my motivations to create and wish for a better life. I have successfully created what I wanted and it all happened because one thing led to another in my life.

For example, I started working a part time job preparing income tax returns for a national income tax preparation company before I did real estate, and while I was still working at the bakery. Then when I least expected, my manager at the tax preparation company asked me if I wanted to do real estate in my spare time because there was a real estate company who was looking to hire Spanish speaking real estate agents. I said yes and I told him I always wanted to be in real estate.

It just did not occur to me that a real estate agent could be a great start. I was still working at the bakery, so I said yes knowing it was a part time job I could do after working at the bakery. One thing lead to another and the rest have just been blessings to my life.

"Don't wish it was easier wish you were better. Don't wish for less problems wish for more skills. Don't wish for less challenge wish for more wisdom" – Jim Rohn

God, or the universe, has all opportunities we need for each one of us. It is up to us to take advantage of those opportunities, and sometimes opportunities come in the form of a problem that needs to be resolved. Problems are God's gift sent to us.

If you have not seen it from this prospective, they are here to make us a better, stronger and wiser version of ourselves.

What I mean is that we are not the same after we have conquered or overcome one of those big problems. I choose to call them challenges in our life, without challenges we will not have the experience or endurance to be a better version of us.

Challenges give that spice to life needed to expect unexpected things. Imagine a life without challenges. How boring would it be? Same old thing every day, knowing what is next every day. Concepts like this are so simple that we take them for granted, we do not think about it or elaborate on it. I personally thank people who have brought me challenges in the past because they have enabled me to seek out a better version of myself.

Now a few years since I left the bakery, I have made much more money working on my business that I could have ever dreamed while working at the bakery. I own my rentals that allow me to have a comfortable life. A few years after I left my job at the bakery my former boss left the bakery too, after his salary was cut and his management title removed.

Life is fair, sooner or later each one of us have our own pay back, positive or negative. If I did not have the problem of someone coming to my world and shaking things up to make me uncomfortable, I may have never become a better version of me and experience all I have experienced in life so far. I have a great life now, I love my life.

I have also experienced life challenges that have enabled me to be more appreciative of the people who really love me and care about me, and not spend much time with the ones who don't. I thank those challenges and differences because I know I am a much better family member now than before due to that.

I heard somebody say something like this, "We spend money we do not have on stuff we do not want just to impress people we do not like," isn't that the truth for some of us? Well it was for me. I personally reversed that, now I spend time and money doing stuff I like with the people I love.

At any level of success we have we will get challenges to that similar level of success, either created by us or by other people who will throw problems at us. It is expected, and the reasons can be many. Tony Robbins once said, "It's easier to bring down the biggest building in the city than build it." So we need to be prepared to conquer problems with a good attitude. Prepare for it. Get our ducks in a row so when challenges arrive or are thrown at us, we are ready to resolve problems and issues with style.

Attitude is everything, it is something we have to work on every day. Challenges are not a thing that will be here for today and once resolved they will go away and will never come back. The same problem may never be back, but I can assure you we will get new ones. It's a fight we have to fight every day, and it's our choice to deal with it with a good attitude or a bad attitude.

The difference is huge. Imagine you have to resolve a work problem. If you do it with a great attitude your chances of making it work are greater that if you choose to do it with a crappy attitude. People like to be around people with great attitudes. Who wants to be around people with bad attitudes? Our persuasion power increases when we have a great attitude.

One of the most important revelations I discovered, that I want to share with you in this final part of the chapter, happened while I was climbing a mountain. I discovered the similarity of the mountain to life. Some of us, we work so hard to get to the top that we forget to enjoy the beauty of the mountain in our journey.

Some, we go on in life without knowing what we really want, led by the illusion that someday, someday we will retire. Someday, when I am rich, someday I will be happy when I achieve, but the reality is that it's an illusion because when we get there we may find out it was not as great as we thought it would be or it was not what we wanted in first place.

The real goal is the journey, the happiness you can experience while obtaining your goals. I ask myself every day what it is that I am thankful for today. That is the most powerful tool you can use to uplift your spirit, attitude and self-esteem because it makes you realize that you actually have things in life many other people don't and you are in much better shape than many others.

Some people do not even have food to eat themselves, let alone food to feed their children. I cannot even imagine how painful that must be. So whenever you are sad, depressed or feel that life is not giving you your fair share, look around and think that there are always people in worse situations than you.

If you'd like to learn about investment opportunities I am I am investing in, learn more about how to increase your investment rate of return or just to get a hold of me, go to my website at Davidsbookclub.com and contact me.

If you felt I was able to contribute something positive to your life in this chapter please share it with someone you care about. Do not keep it secret, and remember that the more you give the more you get.

Thanks for getting this far in this chapter. This is the first time I have ever written a chapter for a book, and I would feel totally privileged to know you have finished. I wrote it with the purpose of contributing back what life has given me. My hope is that I was of service to you and I can help solve any challenge.

My Dedication

I want to dedicate this chapter to all the important people in my life who shared their life with me as contributions and life experiences that have brought me where I am today. Special dedication to my lovely wife Gabriela Quiroz, my son David for whom I mainly wrote this chapter as part of the life learnings I plan on passing on to him and whom I love deeply, and to my mother Arcelia Flores and my brothers and sisters, Rafael, Juan Carlos, Eduardo, Vanessa Monserrat, Deysi and Dian, along with my uncle Luis Aguilar and my aunt Mireya Martinez.

Special thanks to my mentors and teachers from whom with their teachings led me to write this chapter: Dave Lindahl, Jim Rohn, Craig Proctor, Darren Hardy, Tony Robbins, Zig Ziegler, Brian Tracy, Dan Kennedy, Napoleon Hill, Dale Carnegie, Oprah Winfrey, Paulo Coelho, PSI Seminars, Landmark Worldwide and too many more to name on this space.

If you have a positive comment or suggestion on my chapter that you want to share with me, send me a message.

Nothing will make me happier than knowing that my life made a positive difference in someone else's life. You can find my contact information at Davidsbookclub.com There you will find a way to get a hold of me and friend me on Facebook.

PS. Don't forget to get your report "The Most Profitable Landlord's U.S Cities" It's free, just go to Davidsbookclub.com or call my office at 408-333-9767

ADVANCED FINDING FUNDING
Strategy Guide

By SAUL ALARCON

Why do you need to be proactive about finding private money? Money is the lifeblood of your real estate operation. If you do not have access to funding you will not be able to move forward on deals. At some point, the money you currently have or the funds you are able to borrow from the bank will run out. Private money can be the solution and become a very consistent source of funding for you. As you develop and grow your relationships, because real estate investing is a relationship business, more funds will become available to you. So there is no better time than now to ensure you are doing what you can to secure additional sources of funding.

Let me give you an example. When was the last time you were at a real estate auction or foreclosure auction? Did it seem like the same people are buying all of the houses? Do you think they have bank secured mortgages on all of the properties that they just purchased? No, they are able to do these deals because they have the cash, and this cash can be in the form of private money partners. They are staying outside of the lending institutions to fund their deals. This gives them power over you and the other real estate investors in the room. What if you had this same power? What would your real estate career look like today if you could go to the foreclosure auctions, the "as is" auctions, and purchase the properties that fit into your real estate business without the hassle of a mortgage? You need private money so you can get more deals and be competitive in the marketplace. Private money gives you enormous power. Raising private money will certainly take you to another level and allow you to make larger profits.

Having unlimited amounts of capital at your disposal gives you the ability to purchase land, buildings, single family homes, multi-family homes, and buy them at significant discounts. When a seller needs to sell and there is a need to get out of their current situation, they may not have the time to wait for you to secure a mortgage that could take 30-45 days to process. Are you just letting these deals go by? What if you found a property on 123 Emerging Street and the seller was losing their job, was behind on payments (pre-foreclosure) but had some equity in the property. Since they are behind on payments the banks will not refinance. A lender won't take the risk. If you had the cash you could pay off their current loan, any liens or judgments, and maybe even negotiate a short sale because you have the cash to get the lender to discount the note and move the seller on their way.

What if you found a great deal in a decent neighborhood owned free and clear and the seller needs out now? Well, you could structure a purchase agreement and assign it to another investor making yourself a few thousand dollars or you could raise private money and purchase it at a discount. So instead of the person you were going to assign it to making all the money, now you and your investors make all of the money.

What Can You Use Private Money For?

You can use private money to purchase any type of property that you want in your business. You can use private money to fund:

• Residential Properties • Shopping Centers • High-Rise Office Buildings • Speculative Land • New Construction • Rehabbing Old Properties • Government Projects • Industrial Plants

Whatever property or investment strategy you are utilizing can benefit from private money. Let's review some of these a little more closely:

Residential Properties – Apartments have been considered good investments and have provided spendable returns ranging from 4% to 15% (depending on tenant quality and location). Some of the major drawbacks of these properties are that they do require considerable management and they are subject to downturns in the local market. Generally speaking, there is a demand for rental property and you can usually keep them rented out. If you have highly leveraged the property and there is an economic downturn, you could face some problems.

As often as possible, it makes sense to raise enough capital to purchase the property without any debt service. That way, you can manage the property better in times where there are high vacancies. If you get caught in a market where there is little demand for rental properties, owning the building outright will help you be in a financial position to weather the storm until the market changes.

Aside from the spendable income, residential properties have also provided appreciation value over the years. When you factor this with the tax deductions that they provide, it can be a good thing for a syndicate. Some apartment buildings also offer the opportunity for a condominium conversion.

Shopping Centers – The centers are usually offered with national tenants paying a substantial portion of the rent to cover the taxes and mortgage payments. One of the reasons investors like shopping centers is that the tenants are usually long-term tenants with more stability. The major risk is losing one of your anchor tenants as it may take a while to replace them.

There is usually minimal appreciation and very little tax benefits with shopping centers. If you were pooling funds for this type of an investment, you would want to target people that would be interested in a good income with lower risk. This type of investment would likely appeal to retired people, pension funds, or others looking for minimal risk.

High-Rise Office Buildings – There is a specialization in managing these properties that is required in order to be successful at it. This type of investment should only be attempted by an organization with the depth of management experience that can handle this investment. Yields are generally quite high on this type of property. Appreciation also increases on high-rise buildings because of the increasing replacement costs.

Since businesses are the ones that will be your tenants in these buildings, you will generally have longer-term tenants and this offers stability to the investment for those involved. When you have your anchor tenants in place, the risk factor goes down dramatically.

Speculative Land – Land can offer a high degree of leverage because it can be purchased and controlled with minimal money out of pocket. This could be in the form of a small down payment or an option fee. If you select the right piece of land, the returns can be very lucrative. However, a great deal of skill is needed to select the right investment or else you are just gambling.

Since land is a speculative investment, people who invest in this type of property normally use all cash for their purchases. This way, they can reduce their holding costs as they wait for the right opportunity to sell the land or develop it.

New Construction – When the syndicate is involved in new construction, it should receive a larger spendable income to compensate for the higher risk. If you are in a rising rental market, returns can be around 9% or more once the project is completed.

You do need to check with the city planner before taking on this kind of a project. You want to see how many building permits have been issued and what types of jobs are coming into the area. If you build when demand is low and there are not jobs coming into the area, the project will be difficult. Make sure the market conditions are right for this type of an investment project before you commit your money to the deal.

Rehabilitation of Older Properties – There are some syndicates that specialize in finding properties that need renovation and then they will do the work. Because the property is in poor condition, these properties can usually be purchased at a substantial discount. Once the work is done, the value of the property will increase significantly.

The major risk associated with this type of property is the varying costs of the materials and labor for the renovation. It will require a certain amount of skill to find someone that has experience in estimating the repairs and knowing what to budget. When you purchase a property with high vacancy rates, you can also buy the property at a discount.

Government Projects – Government projects offer several advantages. First of all, since you are doing something for the government, it will be much easier to get anything done through the city that is needed. Whether it is rezoning, getting permits, or whatever else is needed for the project, they are going to help you since you are doing the project on their behalf.

The other major benefit to these projects is that funding is usually made readily available. There are often grants and other funds set aside for these projects. This means that you can leverage as much as you possibly can on these projects.

Industrial Plants – Industrial properties may consist of a single tenant with a long-term lease, a multi-tenant industrial building, or an industrial tract for development. These properties generally require much less when it comes to management and supervision. But, it does require someone that has an industrial specialization.

There is one additional challenge that you must be aware of when dealing with industrial properties. Environmental issues require additional due diligence when you are researching the project.

In markets where residential and commercial markets are struggling, industrial could be a good opportunity. There is always at least one segment in the market where you can make a profit regardless of the market conditions. It is a matter of doing your research to find the right opportunity based on the market trends.

It is important to find the right opportunities as a real estate investor. When you are raising money to fund your deals, other investors are going to be looking for deals that will be a good return on their money. The better you are at finding profitable deals, the easier it will be for you to find other people that want to invest their money with you.

That is why it is so important for you to understand that there are always opportunities to make money in real estate regardless of what is happening in the market. If residential real estate is struggling, there could be opportunities in the commercial, land, or industrial segments of the market. Make sure that you do your due diligence in researching what is happening in the market and these opportunities will jump out at you.

If you want to know more about what is happening in the area, I recommend you spend some time with your local city planner. They will have a master plan of what they see happening in the area in the next five years. The city planner can also tell you about new businesses that are coming into the area, what types of jobs they are creating, and how much those people will make. This will help you get a good idea as to what the demand in the area will be.

This is extremely valuable information as you are considering different investment opportunities in the area. The city planner is a very valuable asset and can help you make a lot of money when you know what is happening with real estate in the area.

Primary Investment Objectives

When it comes to investing, people usually invest in order to accomplish one of three outcomes. It is important for you to understand these outcomes, as it will help you target the right people with the deal you have to offer. We will explain how to target people in chapter 6. The main investing objectives are:

1. **Growth** – People will invest their money because they want to make it grow. Growth strategies are those that

will increase your money in lump sums. In real estate, growth strategies would include rehabbing, wholesaling, and also the benefits of property appreciation. All of these strategies are based on the principle of growth investing.

2. **Income** – There are people that will invest their money in order to provide them with a residual income. Many people use this investing outcome as a method of supplementing their retirement, or even using the generated income as a way of paying their monthly expenses so that they are not dependent on the income of a job. The real estate techniques that would provide income would be long-term rentals, lease options, or collecting payments on notes owed to you.

3. **Tax Shelter** – The final outcome is when people invest money in order to pay less money in taxes. As a real estate investor, you need to have a qualified accountant that can help you with strategies to legally reduce the amount of money you pay in taxes. The accountant can advise you as to different ways to reduce your taxable income and there are investments with the specific purpose to provide tax benefits. In real estate, these tax benefits come in the form of depreciation on a rental property, 1031 exchanges, and other techniques.

One of the greatest things about real estate is that you can potentially achieve all three investing outcomes on the same investment. As an example, let's say that you were going to purchase a property with the intention of holding it as a long-term rental. You would achieve the growth outcome as the property values appreciate over time. You would receive income from the rent payments each month. Finally, you would be able to claim depreciation on the property and obtain the tax advantages of owning rental property.

These are a few of the reasons that real estate is such a powerful investment vehicle. Since real estate is such a great investment vehicle, this is the same reason that you need to understand private financing and how it works. These are the reasons that other people will want to invest in the deals that you find. When you have investment opportunities that will help these people achieve their investing goals, you will be able to fund any type of deal.

If you are relying completely on mortgage lenders for all of your loans, then you are going to be limited as to what you can accomplish as a real estate investor. As you continue to acquire properties, there will come a time when lenders will stop providing you loans on properties. That is why you must have a strategy to raise private funds. It will be these private funds that will allow you to achieve more as an investor.

Advantages in Using Private Money

There are many advantages for us as a real estate investor to use private money financing.

• The private money is going to be based on the asset. The investors that will be investing money will be looking for a good deal where they can get a return on their money. Although they will be considering whether or not you have the ability to manage the deal and the property, they will be primarily looking at how their money will be coming back.

• The funds for private money are not going to be based on your credit. Many people do not have credit sufficient enough to purchase the properties they are working on. One of the best advantages of using private money is that your credit will not be a factor. As you are raising private money, the investors will consider your ability to structure a profitable deal and your credit will not be a factor that is considered.

• There will be times with private money where you can raise 100% of the money required for the purchase. This means that you will have the necessary funds for the deal without having to make a down payment. This is a huge benefit over traditional lenders in obtaining a mortgage. Many mortgage lenders would require that you put 10-30% down as a down payment before they would give you a loan. Depending on how you structure the deal, you would be able to avoid the large down payment requirements that would usually be required.

• Private money deals can be closed faster than a traditional loan. A mortgage lender would normally take 30-45 days to review everything prior to getting a final approval from the underwriter. You will likely run into deals where you are going to need to close quickly in order to make the deal work. If you are reliant on traditional funding for all of your deals, you may miss some deals because you would not be able to close quickly enough. Using private money as a funding source will open up opportunities to deals that you would have had to pass on otherwise.

• You can also protect your credit score. If you are raising private money to use equity financing on a deal, you will not be using your credit and so your credit score will also be protected.

• Private money can help you fund larger deals that you would not be able to do on your own without it. Putting together a syndicate is one way that you can pool funds from other investors and use that money to purchase properties that are more expensive.

• There are many ways to profit from raising private funds through syndication. You can make money from the cash flow of the building, from selling the property, a syndication fee for organizing the whole transaction, or even a management fee for running the property during the syndication.

Raising private capital is one true way of capitalizing on your knowledge. Whether you are raising funds from individuals or putting together a syndicate, you are providing an opportunity to make money to other investors. Other investors are always looking for other investment choices that will provide them with a healthy return.

Your job as an investor is to ensure that you are securing profitable deals. If the investor cannot make money on the deal, you are going to have a difficult time raising money.

As you are starting your investing career raising private capital, you must first think of yourself as a transaction coordinator. Your ability to be successful in raising money will be directly related to the deals that you are negotiating. Investors love opportunities to make more money and when you provide them with a deal with a great return, investors will provide you with the investment to make the deal happen.

Even though the point is to demonstrate how to raise private money, you must understand first that finding the right deal is the critical element that will make this process work.

When you have deals that will generate a return on their money to offer to other investors, the money will come.

Summary

Before I can tell you about raising private capital, you must realize that your success in raising money will largely be related to your ability to find good deals. People want to invest their money in deals that will make them more money. Your job is to find those opportunities. As you become skilled in finding good deals, you will find that money will begin to come to you without much effort. Word of mouth will spread as your investors talk to their friends and family about the money they are making through your opportunities.

In order to find profitable deals, you need to realize the potential investing opportunities. There are many different types of properties that you could raise money to purchase. All of them have their benefits and disadvantages. The key is to know which ones make the most sense for your market. The city planner can help you identify these opportunities.

Finally, you must know that every investor is different. They all have different investing objectives. Some of them are looking for growth of their money. Others want to provide income. And yet others are looking for tax advantages. This is important because you need to be able to put yourself in their shoes. When you can find a deal that provides them with their desired investment objective, your success will increase dramatically.

The process I want you to understand is very simple:

1. The right deals will attract money 2. Every market has at least one segment of real estate that is profitable 3. Match the deal with investors looking for that type of investment objective When you line these points up, you have taken the first step in being able to successfully raise capital to run your real estate investing business.

Types of Private Money

Now, I am going to discuss the two different types of private money partners, debt partners and equity partners. Each type of partner will provide different options for putting together a deal. In order to utilize partners as effectively as possible, you will need to be able to present them with viable investment opportunities. If you do not have a profitable deal, finding partners (debt or equity partners) will be difficult.

I am going to describe how each type of partner works and give an example of how you might structure a deal with each type of partner. With this type of format, you can get a detailed idea of how each works and why you would use either a debt or equity partner.

Before we get started on the different types of private money partners it is very important to understand that I will be guiding you on how to talk to individuals to raise private funds for your real estate investment business. It is critical for you to not only understand how these arrangements work, but you must also understand the regulations associated with raising private capital.

In many cases, you will be subject to following the Securities and Exchange Commission guidelines if you are pooling funds from other investors. If you do not follow the guidelines, then you are subject to their consequences.

Debt Partners

A debt partner is an investor who is willing to invest his or her money for a percentage of return on their money. The person that is providing the money will not have any kind of ownership in the deal. Their expectation is that you will pay them a return on their money in the form of interest over the life of the loan.

A debt partner is a situation just like if you were to go to the bank and get a loan. The only difference is that the funder of the loan will be a private party instead of a financial institution.

There are a lot of advantages for you to set up this type of financial arrangement:

• You will not need to approach a financial institution for a loan. There will be times when lenders will give loans very easily and there will be times where lenders do not give many loans. By having a private financing source in the form of a debt partner, you will be able to purchase properties regardless of how lenders are running their businesses.

• In most cases, you will not need to use your credit. Private funders will usually not look at your credit. They are looking at the deal as the vehicle for the return on their money more than they are looking at your creditworthiness.

• Private funders do not usually charge you fees for using their money. Traditional lenders will usually charge you points, origination fees, etc. when you use their money to fund a deal. Many private funders will not require this.

• You will also be able to close a deal more quickly than you would be able to with a traditional lender. This speed can be a very advantageous aspect of private money.

The easiest way to show you how this works is to provide you with an example. The example will also show you what is in the deal for the private investor that is putting up the money on the deal.

Debt Partner Example:

In this example, let's say that you found a great income property and needed $500,000 to purchase the deal. For this example, we are also going to assume that the deal will be profitable for you to purchase. My intent is not to show you the return you would make on the deal. I want to show you how debt partners work and what is in the deal from their point of view.

Purchase Price $500,000 Amount Borrowed $500,000 Loan Interest Rate 9% Loan Period 30 Years Monthly Mortgage Payment $4023.11

With this being the terms of the loan for the debt partner, let's take a look and see what happens for the partner over a five-year period.

Over five years the debt partner would receive payments totaling $241,386.60 ($4023.11 times 60 months = $241,386.60). When you run these numbers through a mortgage calculator, it will show you that $220,787.46 of the total payments was interest on the loan. That means the loan balance is still $479,400.68 after five years of payments.

After five years, the debt partner has received $220,787.46 in interest on their $500,000 investment. This represents a 44% return on their money over these five years ($220,787.46 divided by $500,000 = 44%). This is basically the 9% return each year for the debt partner.

With this quick example, let me review with you why this is a good deal for the debt partner:

• Generating a 9% return each year is a great investment for them. When you consider other places they could invest their money, (money market, certificate of deposit, stock market, mutual funds) this is a much larger return than what they would be able to find elsewhere.

• Their investment has collateral. If the person buying the property were to stop making payments, the debt partner would have a mortgage on the property that would allow them to foreclose and secure the property to secure their investment.

• Their investment is safer than other investment vehicles. This is primarily because real estate is not as volatile as other types of investments.

• By partnering with the person buying the property, the debt partner can invest their money without having to worry about managing the property or knowing anything about real estate. It allows them a "hands off" investment opportunity.

The likelihood of the loan going the full 30 years is quite small. Chances are that the property would be sold or refinanced at some point during the life of the loan. In fact, if you were working with a debt partner that needed to have their money back in five years, you could add a balloon payment to the loan. The balloon payment is a clause in the promissory note that says that any amount still owed on the loan at the end of the agreed upon time period (five years in this example) is owed as one payment. This would allow you five years to either sell the property or locate another source of financing. Balloon payments are a way to allow your debt partner an opportunity to recoup their money without waiting for 30 years.

But just for the sake of example, if the loan were to go the full 30 years, the total interest that would be paid on the loan would be $948,320.68. Keep in mind that is just interest, as it does not account the repayment of the $500,000 principle. This is a great return on their $500,000 investment.

Ideally, a loan from a debt partner would cover the entire purchase price. If it will not cover the entire purchase and you are planning on getting the rest of the money from a traditional lender, you will need to make sure that the lender will subordinate the loan or this situation may not work out for you.

This is why debt partners work and how it is a mutually beneficial relationship. You are offering them an opportunity to make more money in a pretty safe vehicle and you have the opportunity to profit from the deal itself.

Equity Partners

An equity partner is similar to a debt partner but rather than looking for a specific interest rate as a return on their investment, they are interested in a share of the cash flow and the appreciation. Since equity partners are interested in the cash flow they are looking for a minimum of 6-9% cash on cash return going into any deal. Equity partners will also be paid monthly or quarterly based on their percentage and cash flow of the property.

The goal of every deal would be to get a 50/50 split between yourself and the investors. If the numbers are not quite there then slide the investor number up (55/45, 60/40, 65/35, etc.) but never have your percentage lower than 25%. There is too much work that goes into syndicating the deals, raising the private money and managing the deals after they are closed to take less than 25%. Equity partners are also looking for deals that provide a 20% or more annualized return on their investment. This is not a monthly or yearly return but rather the returns on the whole deal.

For example; if you have a three-year deal that provides cash on cash returns of 8% the first year, 9% the second year, 10% the third year for a total of 27% combined return. In year three you sell the property and make a 37% return on the resale. For the three-year period this is a 64% total return. To get the annualized return, divide the 64% by three years and you get 21% as the cash on cash return. This is what your equity investors are looking for when they invest.

Here is another way to look at it:

Summary of Projected Owner Cash Flow and Returns
Initial Equity
$3,150,000 Year 1 Year 2 Year 3 Return $ Return %

Owner net Cash Flow

 $286,873 $284,150 $289,553 $860,576

Cash on Cash Return

9.10% 9.02% 9.19% 27.31%

Owner Equity

   $1,051,500 33.40%

Total Return on Investment

   $1,912,076 60.71%

Annualized Return

   20.23%

In order to ensure annualized returns you need to go through a process called the carve out. The carve out is the amount of ownership that you can carve out of a deal for yourself. Since the investors are putting up all of the money for the deal and their expectation is to have a percentage of the cash flow and appreciation, you need to ensure that you calculate the numbers for every deal very carefully.

One way to calculate your carve out is by utilizing "the trinity."

The trinity is three different numbers or ratios, that when they fall into line, allow you to carve out 25% or more of the deal for yourself. You get the acquisition fee and 25+% of the cash flow and appreciation. Before we go into the trinity, let us take a moment to explain the acquisition fee and how it is involved in your private money transactions. The acquisition fee is an industry standard fee of 1-5% of the purchase price that you can receive for sponsoring the deal. You are considered the sponsor because you found the deal, brought together the investors, and are managing the deal. At the closing table you will receive a check for the acquisition fee. Private money investors have an expectation to pay this fee. In theory, you could get into a deal with absolutely no money out of your pocket and be paid at the closing table.

Partner Summary

We covered a lot of terms and ideas in the last few pages. Let's take just a moment to summarize these so that you have a full understanding as we move forward.

Debt Partner: No equity participation. Functions very much like a bank and expects a percentage return on their investment. Paid at the time of resale or refinancing.

Equity Partner: Participates in a portion of equity. Participates in cash flow. Participates in all proceeds from the resale.

Cash on Cash Return: A percentage that reflects your return on investment based on the money you had to pay out of pocket to get involved in the deal. This is calculated by taking the money made on the deal and dividing by the money invested.

Acquisition Fee: Is an industry standard fee of 1-5% of the purchase price that you can receive for putting together the real estate investment deal.

Carve Out: The percentage of ownership that you will retain in the deal. This should be no lower than 25%.

The Trinity

As we mentioned earlier, the trinity are the three different numbers, or calculations, or ratios that you will look at to determine if you can carve out at least 25% cash flow to syndicate a deal with your investors. The three calculations are based on capitalization rate, cash on cash return, and debt coverage ratio. We will look at each of these individually to demonstrate how they are used to create your carve out. Before we analyze each area of the trinity we need to define some of the terms that will be used in their calculations.

1. Net Operating Income (NOI) – This is the income on a property after expenses, but excluding your mortgage. You can increase your NOI by decreasing expenses or increasing income. NOI = Yearly Income – Yearly Expenses

2. Operating Expenses – Expenses that occur on a recurring basis, such as taxes, insurance, repairs and maintenance.

3. Capital Expenses – Those expenses that you will depreciate; such as a new roof, carpet and appliances.

4. Acquisition costs – This is your down payment (20 – 30%), your closing costs (3%) and your acquisition fee (1-5%). In other words, this is the capital it will require you to purchase the property. The capitalization rate (cap rate) is the return that you expect to get on your investment. It is calculated by taking your Net Operating Income (NOI) divided by the Sales Price or the value of the property. The cap rate that you are looking for needs to be above 7.75%. Many traditional lenders require that the cap rate be at least that high or they will not even consider financing the deal.

Cap Rate = NOI/Sales Price

Purchase Price $6,200,000 Net Operating Income $675,000
Cap Rate 10.8%

Neighborhoods are also a good indicator of cap rates. Keep in mind that you should still run your numbers and not rely on location to make your investment decisions.

• "A" neighborhoods consist of buildings that were built in the last 10 years and might have a cap rate of 6-7%. • "B" neighborhoods were built about 25 years ago and might have a cap rate of about 8-9%.

• "C" neighborhoods would consist of buildings built about forty years ago but are still in good condition. The properties, if maintained, can still build appreciation. These properties might have a cap rate of 10-11%. • "D" neighborhoods are properties that might have a cap rate of 12%+ and are typically in neighborhoods referred to as "war zones". These are the properties that you and your private partners will want to stay away from.

These are all factors that you need to consider when evaluating the type of property that you want to offer to your partners. They are going to have certain types of investments in mind and you want to make sure that the type of property matches their investment objectives.

The cash on cash return evaluates what percentage of the money you have invested is going to come back to you as investment income. As a quick example, if an investor were to invest $150,000 and made $75,000 in the first year from that money, the cash on cash return for the investor would be 50%. Here is the formula and an example of how to calculate the cash on cash return.

Cash on Cash Return = NOI – Debt Service /Acquisition cost
Net Operating Income $460,000 Debt Service $350,000
Acquisition Cost $875,000 Cash on Cash Return 12.6%

This cash on cash return needs to be at 12% or higher in order for you to syndicate. If it is less than this, your investors will likely look to other investment opportunities. The debt coverage ratio allows you to see how many times the cash flow will cover the mortgage. This calculation is very important to understanding if the property can produce enough income to cover the debt. Remember that anything above the mortgage is profit. Typically a lender would want to see a debt coverage ratio of about 1.2 to 1.3. This calculation allows you to see if the property is healthy. Debt Coverage Ratio = NOI/Debt Service
Net Operating Income $600,000 Debt Service $350,000 Debt Coverage Ratio 1.71

This debt coverage ratio needs to be at 1.6 or higher for you to syndicate the deal.

When you have completed all of your calculations, your trinity should look something like this: Cap Rate: 8+ Cash/Cash Return: 12+ Debt Coverage Ratio: 1.6+

With these numbers in alignment you will be able to create deals with a carve out of 25%. This means you will get 25% of the cash flow and the equity. Also, you will have received your acquisition fee of 1-5% of the purchase price at closing. If the numbers are not in alignment, then you may have to adjust the numbers slightly to keep investors interested, or you may need to find a different property. Remember that your ability to keep investors interested is going to be completely based on the deal. Everything hinges on your ability to present the investors with a deal where the numbers make sense to them.

Types of Private Money Deals

To be successful in real estate investing you have to be able to secure good deals for your private money partners. The two different types of deals that you need to become familiar with are momentum plays and repositioning plays. As you will notice, each deal provides a different payment structure to your investors. In a momentum play, the properties already have cash flow at the time of closing. There is nothing you need to do to get the properties ready for tenants.

After the closing, you hand it over to your management company and you and your partners reap the benefits of cash flow, month after month. In this type of deal your carve out should be a minimum of 25%. In a repositioning play you are upgrading the property and you are upgrading the tenant base. This is a very risky investment strategy as there will be little to no cash flow during the first year and the cash on cash return will always be zero. The reason the cash on cash return remains at zero is because you want to put any additional income into construction costs. As construction costs can vary, you will need to reserve the monthly income for these expenses. When the deal is done then you can pay the cash flow to the investors.

Although there are downsides to the repositioning play, there are also upsides as well. Keep in mind that with multi-family buildings, the value of the property is based on the income. If the property has a lot of vacancies, this means that the property could be purchased at a discount because of the lower cash flow. One of the easiest ways to increase the value of a multi-family building is to increase the cash flow. As the cash flow rises, so does the value of the property.   In this type of deal, you want to look for a 25% annualized return because of the risk involved. Also, you should have no more than 30% of our portfolio in repositioning plays because of the risk involved.

Due to this risk, and the management involved, you will want to have a minimum carve out of 50%. Keep in mind that the two reasons most repositioning plays fail is because the money runs out or the wrong management company is hired.

How Financing Affects the Project

In many cases, two things usually determine the success of the project:

1. Your acquisition strategy 2. The financing that is secured

Therefore, your success in raising capital for your deals is best spent in these two areas. When you focus your time on how you purchase the property (the price, the terms, etc.) and how the project is going to be financed, you will receive the greatest return on your time that is possible.

The acquisition strategy is critical because you are going to lock in the money on the deal depending on how you buy it. When you buy a property at the right price with the right terms, you have secured the profit on the deal. There is an expression in real estate investing that says that you make your money when you buy. This expression is only partially true. The profit is secured when the property is acquired the right way.
However, the profit is realized once it is acquired and rented, resold, etc. But you cannot realize a profit on the deal

when the property is not purchased the right way. Since you are locking in the profit when you purchase the property, it is critical to ensure that you are buying a good deal. The formulas will help you determine whether your project is a good deal or not.

Since we are focusing on financing and different types of funding, it is also important to understand how financing is going to affect the project that you are working on. Loan payments can have a positive or negative effect on the spendable income of the deal. The spendable income is the amount of cash flow remaining after paying the debt service. Why is financing and the net spendable income so important?

• Many investors are cash flow oriented. They want to know what cash they will receive in comparison with the amount of money they need to invest to receive that cash flow. That is why you need to understand the trinity calculations. These formulas will help you to lock up a deal that will make the investors want to be involved.

• Many investors do not factor in mortgage reduction as a contributing factor to their investment in the deal. As mortgage payments are being made, the loan balance decreases (assuming you have a fully amortized loan). However, inflation is usually rising as well and it is eroding the equity that is gained by paying down the loan over time. This is another reason that the net spendable income on the property is king for most investors.

• Although some investors invest for the purpose of tax benefits, this cannot always be counted on. Tax rules are constantly changing and one decision by congress can quickly erode the tax benefits associated with real estate. When the government needs to increase the tax revenue they receive, you could see them reduce the tax benefits received by investors. Tax benefits should be considered an added benefit of the investment instead of being the only reason to invest in a deal.

• Fluctuating interest rates can have a negative impact on the returns if you have a mortgage payment with a fluctuating rate.

These points should help you see into the thoughts of the investors that are going to invest their money with you. In order to be successful with raising capital and providing investment opportunities to other people, you have to know about the issues on their mind, and how financing is going to affect the profits on your deal.

Factors to Consider for Financing

In order to decide where to go for financing, you must understand the factors involved that will affect your decision on where to turn. Keep in mind that raising private money is not going to be the best option for every single deal.

There are going to be times when going to the bank and getting a loan is going to make the most sense for your project. There will also be times when the bank will not loan you money and so you are going to need to know other ways of putting the deal together.

With that in mind, the best source for financing a particular project will depend on the following information:

A. The equity that the borrower has. Some lenders are willing to lend a higher percentage of value than others.
B. The length of the loan. Some sources offer longer time periods on their loans than other lenders.

C. Type of property. Loan terms will be different if the property is residential or commercial.

D. The quality of the cash flow. Sources will differ greatly in how competitive they are depending on the quality of the income on the property. This is true for traditional lenders as well as private funders.

E. Geographic location. Some lenders have restrictions on the areas where they loan money.

F. Amount of the loan. Each lender has a maximum loan limit that they cannot go beyond. If the deal is larger than what they are capable of loaning, they will either refer it out to another lender, or they will put together a loan syndication and get other lenders to go in on the deal with them.

When you are putting together a deal and you are working on the financing for the project, you have to understand how these factors will impact your ability to get a loan or whether it makes more sense to raise private capital.

If you are finding lenders that are not able or willing to finance the project, then you will need to find another alternative and private money is one way of doing it. The private money you raise could come in the form of a debt partner or an equity partner.

The main point that I want to make is that there is not one lending solution (traditional lender, hard money lender, private money etc.) that is going to work in every single situation. Each situation is unique and every deal is different. That means you must find the best alternative for each deal. Each type of financing will also have an impact on the profitability of the deal because of the cost of obtaining the money.

Summary

I hope that this helps you to see the vision of private money. When you are putting together a deal where you will be using other investor's money, you have to understand that factors that they are thinking about. Outlined above are some very important principles that you need to master:

• How to put together a deal with either a debt or equity partner. At this point, you should know what the difference is and what each type of partner is looking for. You should also know how to explain what type of return they would receive under either type of partnership.

• The trinity calculation is a key for helping you line up the deal to the point where other investors will want to be a part of the offering. The formulas for the net operating income, the cash on cash return, debt coverage ratio, and the capitalization rate will be important guidelines for you to structure your deal.

• There are many factors that involve how a deal will be financed. These are points that you should be considering as you are evaluating a deal.

• Negotiating a good carve out is an important part of making money through syndicating. This is compensating you for your time and effort of putting the deal together.

• Above all else, remember that your ability to raise capital is also going to be linked to your ability to structure a good offering. When the deal is profitable, investors will jump at the opportunity to make more money.

These points will build your foundation for raising private capital. At this point, I need to discuss the legal ramifications of pooling funds from other investors before I teach you the "how" of raising private money.

Locating Private Money Sources

Locating private money partners is not as difficult as you may think. As we discussed in the previous chapter it is very important to develop a relationship with any individuals that you have discussed your business with, either through the elevator pitch, a luncheon or a seminar. Therefore, the approach that you take when advertising to potential investors is very important. Do not take this process for granted. You have a lot to lose by not following the guidelines.

It is important to point out that if you are doing a public offering, then you are allowed to advertise freely to the public. If you are doing a private offering under one of the Regulation D exemptions, then you cannot advertise to the general public. You have to target your advertisements to a group of accredited investors, or to people that you already know.

As a syndicator raising private money, you need to create a marketing plan that fits the purpose of the project and the target investor group. You would do well to consider the positive aspects of the project and what types of investors would be interested in your offering. This will allow you to customize the market efforts to the right people in the beginning.

This type of customization will help you attract the right types of investors from the very beginning. Attracting the right investors from the start will cause you a lot less trouble and stress. Some investors may mistakenly give you their money because you were very personable and good at presenting the opportunity, but they may have a change of heart during the deal. How will you react if an investor wants you to buy them out of their position in the deal? The whole point here is to find the right people to begin with so that these types of situations are kept to a minimum.

As an example, let's say that you were assembling an offering that offered a tax shelter as the primary objective of the investment. Remember how we talked about investment objectives (growth, income, tax shelters) at the beginning of the course? If you had this tax shelter offering and started marketing the deal to people looking for income, you are likely wasting your time and money. You would be better served marketing the opportunity to people that are in a high tax bracket and would need the tax shelter to reduce their taxable income.

You must also consider the risk tolerance of investors. Every investor has their own level of risk that they are comfortable with. When marketing your offering to others, think about the type of risk involved in your deal and market that to investors with a similar risk tolerance. Some investors will like higher risk deals like construction or land development deals. Others are more conservative and will be looking for something that provides cash flow.

As you are creating the marketing plan for your project, you must keep these factors in mind in order to reach the right types of investors and maximizing your efforts and money that are invested in marketing.

Also keep in mind that the techniques I share with you in this section are simply things that you could do. Everyone has a specific personality and these techniques are based on different personality types. Some people are comfortable speaking in front of a group. Others are better in a one-on-one setting. Find the techniques that will work well with the type of person you are. If you are uncomfortable talking about the deal, most people will perceive that to mean that you are nervous about the deal. The person you are approaching will begin to feel nervous too. It is important to use the techniques that work well with your style.

Here are some marketing strategies that you can use to find the people to fund your deals:

Direct Personal Contact

The starting point for most syndicators is to compile a list of people that they know who would potentially be interested. This list will consist of family members, friends, business associates, or other relatives. I also recommend that you continue building this list using the networks of your friends and family.

A technique called an elevator pitch is a brief 30 second introduction.

When I am using this method, I use the same technique I outlined in the previous chapter on the elevator pitch. Many people talk to their friends and family the wrong way. When they are asking if they are interested in the deal they are working on, they usually ask the question, "Would you be interested in investing in this deal?"

The problem with this question is that it closes the door if they are not interested. Also, most people do not like to be directly solicited like this. In fact, if you are abrasive in how you ask or you say the wrong thing, you will not only fail to receive the money, but you will damage a relationship in the process. This is the wrong way to approach direct personal contact.

The easier way is to simply change the question that you are asking. Once you have presented the opportunity you are working on, the question I like to ask is, "Who do you know that would be interested in something like this?" By asking the question like this, the person is not put on the spot. They will be able to answer without feeling pressured. If they are interested in the deal, they will speak up and say so.

If they do not have any interest, the question is specifically geared towards having the person think about the people they know. This will allow you to tap into that person's personal network. Most people have connections with people that have money and those people would like an opportunity to make more money.

Third Party Basis

Instead of working with people you directly know (friends, associates, etc.) this technique focuses on using other people that have resources. You want to focus on people that have large resources of people available to them.

People like attorneys, accountants, property managers, real estate brokers, investment advisors, and securities brokers are just a few examples. These people have large lists of people that they work with and many of these people also have money to invest.

You can market your opportunity through these third parties to reach the target market of investors. There are a lot of syndicators that prefer this method because they feel that the third-party recommendation will be more easily accepted by the potential investor than if the syndicator were to present it themselves. The third party already has a relationship of trust with the people that will be offered with the opportunity.

There are many people that raise private funds through these third-party offerings and they specialize their marketing to this technique. Frequently, they will use realtors and/or investment advisors as their primary method of raising capital for the offering.

Using this technique, you would not be required to do any selling. You would mostly be answering any questions the potential investor had, distributing materials like the credibility kit, and the information about the specific offering.

Marketing through these individuals becomes an effective way to market your opportunity and provide investment opportunities to the professional's clients.

The process would consist of educating these third-parties about the offering and providing them with your sales packet of information.

Media Advertising

Many syndicate organizations use media advertising as their primary method of raising investor capital. Depending on the type of advertising that you are doing, this could be a relatively low cost method of raising money for your deals.

You must be careful to ensure that your advertising complies with the guidelines that have been issued by the Securities and Exchange Commission. However, you must find the balance between following the guidelines and making the marketing compelling enough that it generates interest. If you are doing a private offering, you will be limited on the amount of media advertising that you will be able to do.

On your marketing, you cannot state a specific or guaranteed rate of return. Each state also has its own amended laws that you must follow. Make sure you are working with a competent attorney that has experience in syndication.

Some examples of media advertising would be:

Newspaper Advertising

At this point in time in your real estate career you have utilized some form of advertising for selling a home, looking for tenants or just advertising your business in the local newspapers. You can also advertise for private money investors in the newspapers but you have to be very careful of the language that you use. In general, the SEC frowns upon the use of newspapers or other print media to solicit investors, especially when they contain return percentages such as "interested in earning 9% to 15% interest on investments secured by local real estate." The ad can discuss your business but not solicit an investment. An example of an ad you might run is "What does the real estate bubble mean to you? Find out at a luncheon hosted by XYZ Real Estate Company. Call 888-8888888 to reserve your seat." This will bring individuals to your luncheon presentation where you will encourage them to complete the accredited investor form.

Direct Mail

Another form of advertising is a direct mail piece. As with any advertising where you want more than one investor, it needs to be generic in nature. You should purchase a list of qualifying individuals from a mailing list broker. The prices for these names vary by region of the country but $.28 - $.48 per name is a reasonable charge. You will then mail these prospects a postcard inviting them to your next luncheon or seminar.

Many list brokers will be able to provide you with a list of accredited investors that you can send a letter to their home. This list ends up being a good way to do marketing as well as complying with the SEC requirements.

Flyers

Flyers are a very effective way to introduce your business at Real Estate Investment Associations (REIAs) or other social gatherings. Your flyers should have great pictures, bold headlines, and action words and be limited to one page. There are two aspects to creating a flyer that you should be aware of, as the SEC governs general solicitations. There are some things you can do to target one investor that you cannot do to target more than one investor.

Flyers can also be effective at meetings with the chamber of commerce, syndicate groups, or builder or developer associations. A little research on the Internet will help you locate these groups that are closest to your location.

Flyers for single investors: These flyers should only be a one-page description of your deal. Your flyer should always contain your contact information, who you are, and what you do. Be specific as to the types of property that you invest in. Since you are only seeking out one partner you can display a picture of the property and the investment return. When you are marketing to just one investor for one project, you are not syndicating and you are not subject to the SEC regulations. The regulations only apply when you are pooling money from multiple investors. Seeking out one investor makes the rules much easier.

Above all, the flyer should be simple. Make sure it is easy to understand and does not confuse the reader. If the reader is confused they will not know what the action is they should take. Flyers for multiple investors: The flyer for multiple investors is similar to that of the single investor. As with the previous flyer, ensure that it is simple and clear. The flyer for multiple investors should not mention any percentage rates of returns, or locations of property. You can discuss the types of property that you invest in and testimonials from previous investors. Above all, include a call to action to complete your accredited investor form.

Sponsorship By Another Organization

There are syndicators that specialize in working with various professional organizations in offering their opportunities strictly to members of their profession. Some examples would be doctors, attorneys, professors, engineers, airline pilots, etc.

The group will tailor their proposal and marketing efforts to the needs and objectives of these individual groups. As they limit their proposal to these groups, they are adding to the allure of the opportunity by making it "exclusive" to that individual group.

Presentations

Presentations at various events, like REIAs, are a great opportunity to utilize your elevator pitch and excite investors into completing your accredited investor form to get more information. Since your elevator pitch is already compliant with SEC guidelines you do not have to worry about a focus on one investor or multiple investors. As with the luncheon presentation you will get questions about the rate of return or how much money they have to invest. Be sure to answer them with a call to action and setup the second meeting. Even if you do not make a formal presentation you should always be utilizing your elevator pitch when you meet people. Make it a goal to always talk to someone you do not already know on a daily basis. This is a great way to share your business and to collect business cards from those that you meet. Presenting and networking is a basis for developing relationships and again this is a relationship business.

One on One Presentations

Now that you have received accredited investor forms from the people that you met through networking, you need to prepare to meet with them over coffee, lunch or dinner. The presentation that you provide during this meeting is just as critical as any other presentation you have done up to this point. This is your opportunity to shine and review your credibility kit with the investor. Be sure to let them know how they can get involved in your business. Above all, ask them if they are interested in getting involved. If you do not ask the questions, you will not know the answer.

With any presentation we have covered to this point it is very important that you practice each presentation, more than once. These presentations should be as fluid as any conversation that you have with a friend, colleague or spouse. The more confident and comfortable you are with your presentation the more confidence you will display when you are presenting.

Summary

Marketing is a critical component for raising capital. You could have the best opportunity in the world, but it will not matter if people do not know about it. Marketing is the means by which you will attract potential investors to your projects.

Although I have stated it several times, it is important to follow the guidelines set forth by the SEC. There are certain restrictions that you will be under depending on the type of offering you are going to make. Make sure that your marketing plan takes this into account.

Do the type of marketing that works well with your personality. You do not need to be a fantastic public speaker to be successful raising capital. You do not need to be a compelling salesperson to instill confidence in people. The deals you do should do the majority of the talking for you. You should be having deals that are offering a true opportunity to your investors. When this is the case, marketing is nothing more than a way to get the word out about what you have to offer.

Let's Begin Our Relationship!
Contact Me Today

If you're ready to take the step on your way to high net-worth, all you have to do is contact us and we will talk with you about the opportunities.

Telephone: (650)766-4605

Email: salarcon@imfi.us